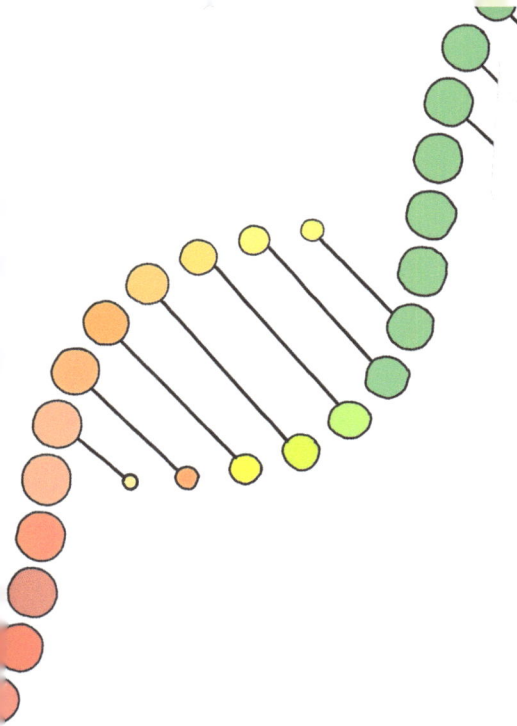

Collaboration in a Digital World

David Jenkins

First published in 2022
Tri Helix

National Library of Australia Cataloguing-in-Publication entry:

Author: Jenkins, David.

Title: Collaboration in a Digital World / David Jenkins

ISBN: 9780994350701

Subjects: Collaboration, leadership, success in business.

To my family and those who collaborated by sharing their valuable time to create this book.

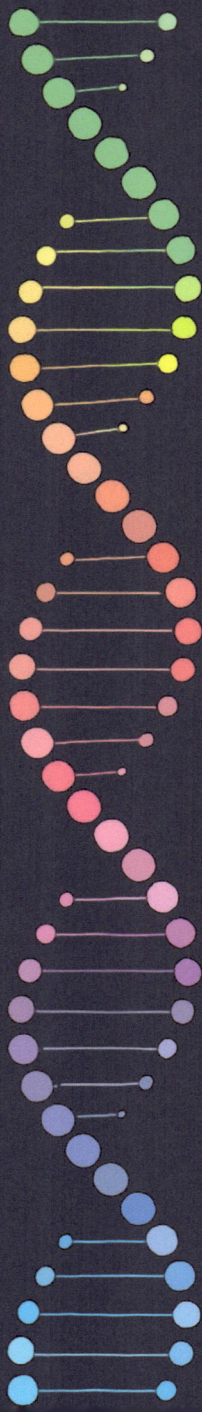

Contents

Foreword

If people are the key to effective and successful outcomes, then collaboration is how we enhance and magnify that success. This book provides insights and lessons on how we collaborate to connect and achieve truly great, breakthrough outcomes, and do it with a thriving team. David has been instrumental in helping my teams and I attain just that. He is a great leader and inspirer of teams working together; an expert in helping whole organisations find clarity, focus and alignment, and now a thought leader in collaboration in a digital world. In writing this foreword, I'm delighted to share some words that I'd always hoped to have the chance to write.

"If people are the key to effective and successful outcomes, then collaboration is how we enhance and magnify that success."

I have a diverse and enviable background, afforded me by a magnificent and generous resources industry that I have been lucky to be a part of. I have lived and worked on six of the seven continents and been employed by small, large, and very large companies producing a broad range of commodities. I have had the opportunity to lead both operations and technical teams, most recently in the Executive Vice President, Division Leader and International Executive Manager roles.

Perhaps most importantly, I've built and led three extremely high-functioning, high-performing teams of extraordinary professionals in delivering breakthrough outcomes for the businesses where we were employed. Of course, full credit lies with the team. As their leader, my role was to find the ways, resources, tools and techniques for them to achieve their very best.

For the past 20 years, David and I have worked together using structured, effective and efficient approaches to deliver work that required multifaceted injections through workshopping. My most recent team was a unique, specialist, high-functioning team that worked from anywhere in the world on anything in the world and in a multi-national and diverse multi-asset business. Our "secret recipe" was to show up! We spent months every year on airplanes delivering work with passion and dedication to our clients and site stakeholders. David and his team's tools and techniques were at the core of some of our best work.

It was about November 2019 when we first heard the dreaded Corona word and there was some commotion building. Initially I did not worry, anticipate or plan for any particularly significant impact. Yet by March 2020, I was being "evacuated" from the UK and I returned to Australia. The world had changed. Initially overwhelmed, we tried to make sense of what was happening and began to see this as an enormous if confronting opportunity, an imperative to re-imagine the way we worked. The new environment compelled us to develop and test innovative and agile approaches for achieving bigger, better and faster outcomes.

Amid all this change, David was about to do some of the most important thinking and development of our entire careers in working together.

"Amid all this change, David was about to do some of the most important thinking and development of our entire careers."

David's journey has taken him from a tradesman (Fitter and Turner) to an engineer (Mechanical), to a Project Manager and now on to helping whole organisations shape their futures. He used his considerable expertise to develop and share key tools and processes, helping whole organisations to connect. His drive to innovate and help people has led him to become a thought leader in new ways of working and the value of collaboration and connection. He embodies the charisma of multiple re-inventions and perhaps, most importantly, the authenticity to bring multi-dimensional success to everything he touches.

"The book is a collation of stories, processes and toolkits for delivering work that integrates teams and stakeholders."

The book is a collation of stories, processes and toolkits for delivering work that integrates teams and stakeholders. It shares lessons about connecting people, no matter where they are, so that they might really understand each other in a way that has them interacting as if in the same room. It communicates the benefits of collaborating digitally by engaging with the best regardless of geography, using digital platforms to enable asynchronous work and enabling new learning and personal growth.

Tri Helix and David have built this work from real data, from face-to-face interviews, surveys and an analysis of deliverables. There are no other "kits" quite like this, just as there are few major organisations truly collaborating virtually to deliver better and stronger outcomes than ever.

This approach can apply to all areas, for example my daughter and her Rhythmic Gymnastics Team represented Australia at the Tokyo Olympics and together illustrated what high performance is all about. Beyond all the practice and preparation is connection, respect and truly wanting the best for each other, stating: "Individually we are all elite athletes, together we are Olympians".

In short, when it comes to your team, one plus one does not necessarily equal two.

The most important thing that you will do as a team or project leader is to influence and engage, communicate options and opportunities, and drive great outcomes in your business. I believe collaboration and connection lie at the core.

"Individually we are all elite athletes, together we are Olympians."

For me, the confidence to trigger this completely new way of achieving outcomes began with my most recent (and perhaps the most magical) team. And it worked. I only asked that my team embrace the change, come on the journey and work with David and our leaders to navigate the landscape to a new norm.

Collaboration and connection have been the upfront injections for every truly successful team that I have witnessed or led. Read this book, familiarise yourself with the material and toolkits. Trust it and use it with your teams and stakeholders. Don't miss your chance to be magnificent.

Dr Carmen Letton

Managing Director and Principal

"Lead your people with love"

"Collaboration is when we are deeply present with one another and the more deeply we are in presence the deeper the collaboration."

Spiritual Leader

Undertaking
the journey

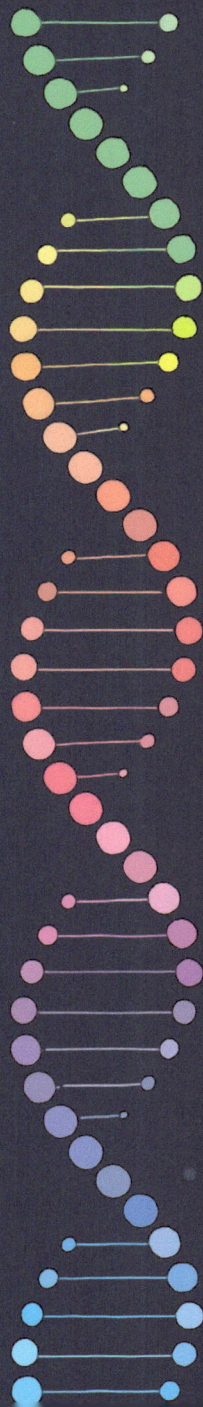

Making the transition to being a successful collaborator has many benefits.

- Imagine collaborating with the best and most diverse people while maintaining a work/life balance with increased autonomy and flexibility.

- Imagine making a difference through faster turnaround and effective work sessions and asynchronously working in real-time across time zones.

- Imagine building a sense of community with shared goals and a larger purpose where people know how to contribute.

- Imagine building lasting and personal connections built on trust and respect.

- Imagine being able to confront unknowns and embrace the digital world with confidence and energy where remote people are fully engaged and the collaboration is timely, cost effective and good for the environment.

As an individual, making the transition to becoming a successful collaborator is necessary as it will happen anyway. With the ongoing development of new technology, we will be exposed to many ways to collaborate.

There will be obstacles and challenges along the way. Taken out of your comfort zone, there will be moments of fear and vulnerability. Sacrifices will need to be made and some old beliefs will have to go. You will need to confront some new situations. This journey may take some time but it's well worth the effort. So, plunge in and get started.

The purpose of this book is to assist you in this important transition in order to produce more successful outcomes. The book shares the results of my investigation into why we collaborate and the threats and rewards faced by collaborators. At its core was research involving conversations with more than 50 people from across 17 industry sectors.

Collaborating
with the best

Making a difference

Building a sense of
community

Building lasting and
personal connections

Embracing the
digital world

Why collaborate

Part 1: Why collaborate

Part 1 reflects on other people's collaboration stories to see how similar we are as we desire to connect and contribute. The experiences of these collaborators are documented and organised into a collaboration DNA. Over 80 collaboration stories are shared and grouped into five key themes describing why we collaborate: it's a law of nature; it makes us feel good; it's powered by people; it's through interactions; it produces outcomes.

Part 2: How to collaborate

Part 2 explains how to collaborate in the digital world, involving campaigns, mantras, essentials, interactions, timelines and threats, rewards and obstacles to collaboration. Each topic is supported with practical tools and techniques to help you make the transition to becoming an effective leader and collaborator.

How to collaborate*

Source: Golden Circle - Simon Sinek

Part 3: What to collaborate on

Part 3 provides an approach to defining what we want to collaborate on, discussing collaboration scope, success, delivery model, scenarios and overall framework. Each topic is supported with practical tools and techniques to help you make the transition to becoming an effective leader and collaborator.

Just remember, collaborating in the digital world is not as hard as you may think.

What to collaborate on

"Collaboration is part of our human design, hardwired into our brains and essential to our survival."

Historian

Part 1 - Why collaborate

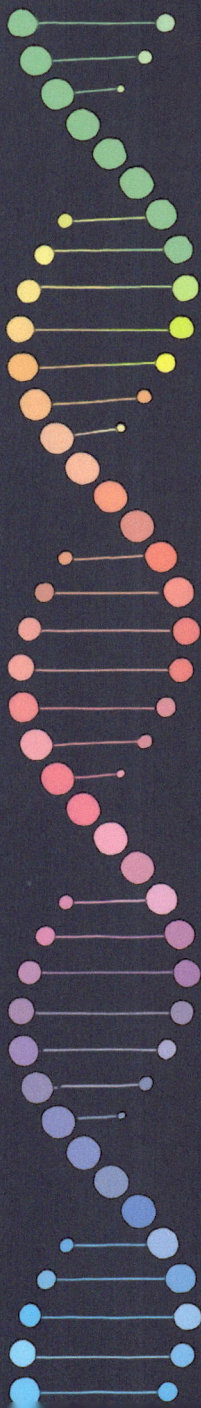

Technology change

Essence of the problem

With the collaboration DNA providing a clear explanation of why we want to collaborate, it's important to understand why we struggle at times.

Our research identified three major threats:

- People are being forced to confront unknowns and deal with technology change. They struggle with digital work fatigue, experience poor relationships and battle technology failure.

- We allow a power imbalance as face-to-face people take control, alienating and ignoring remote participants. They feel second class, frustrated, disconnected, silly and not valued.

- We consume costs, the environment and time. It can be expensive to bring people together as we consume travel costs and CO_2 emissions. It's also difficult to find time slots in people's calendars and consequently we lose momentum or don't get the best people.

Consume costs, the environment and time

Source: Tri Helix Collaboration Training program. 110 obstacles identified from 60 interviews across the world.

Avoiding these threats affects our individual behavior which often leads to making the wrong decisions and common mistakes, for example:

1. Avoiding new technology and resisting change.
2. Believing people only make connections face to face.
3. Treating remote people as second-class citizens.
4. Thinking face to face is always the best approach.
5. Waiting until we get everyone in the same room.

Our research also identified three major benefits of collaborating virtually:

- We can grow and develop with the best and most diverse people in the world. Where you learn, make a difference and reimagine the future while maintaining a work-life balance.

- We can build and foster teamwork across time zones. Everyone can see the big picture by ensuring that remote people with the right skills can contribute.

- We can explore people's emotions to build a cohesive sense of community where people belong. They have deeper personal connections and understand how they contribute.

Most diverse people

Explore people's emotions

Hybrid collaboration

Case study - Collaboration in a digital world

With the onset of COVID, traditional approaches to collaboration stopped overnight. It was no longer possible to meet face to face as people stayed home and dialed in remotely. Like everyone else, we waited and expected it to be a short-term change and before long we would all be back in the office and working as usual.

After a month it became obvious the world was changing. We needed to rethink how we work and pivot collaboration to a virtual world. We quickly signed up to digital whiteboards and Zoom and started to collaborate. Naturally it was not pretty at the start and like many of you, we made mistakes. However, with time and lots of practice we developed a skill set to collaborate virtually. The technology allowed us to go from the ugly to being organised and coordinated in our approach as we solved problems on the run to morph the virtual world into an interactive and incredibly productive space.

As I now reflect on the past two years, I am amazed at what we have achieved. Initially being a skeptic and believing the best way to collaborate is face to face, I now take a more balanced approach and believe most collaboration can be done virtually, while reserving face to face for the critical work of facilitating emotions and connections.

The future of collaboration

In fact, I am working on a collaboration campaign involving 25 people around the world who will attend six virtual sessions leading up to and after a three-day workshop. The infographic on page 19 is a snapshot of this work in terms of time, CO_2 emission and costs avoided in working virtually.

COLLABORATING IN A VIRTUAL WORLD
TIME, CO2 EMISSIONS & BUDGET SAVED

873 Total people

29 Total projects

21 Countries involved

237 Total people avoided international travel

Workshops 2020-2022
Tri Helix

4,757 Total international flight time avoided (hours)

$2,378,407 Total cost of international flights avoided ($AUD)

428,113 Total CO2 emmissions avoided (kg)

1,664,885 Total international flight distance avoided (miles)

International travelling participants averages

7025	20	$10,035	1806
Avg. international flight distance (miles)	Avg. international flight duration (hours)	Avg. cost of international flight ($AUD)	Avg. CO2 emissions (kg)

Source: Tri Helix Virtual Collaboration workshops from 2020 to 2022.

60
INTERVIEWS

270
STORIES

17
SECTORS

30k
WORDS

Collaboration DNA

Recognising "People do not buy what you do, they buy why you do it" – Simon Sinek. It was important to understand why people collaborate, what's their purpose or belief. Why do they want to interact with others? More importantly, why do people want to collaborate at all?

To answer these questions, I interviewed 50 people from 17 sectors and simply asked 'why do we collaborate'. The responses were diverse and insightful and filled me with hope and joy in humanity.

It became apparent early on that when you go beyond the obvious of doing things better, some common themes appear showing that collaboration is built deeply into our psyche and is necessary to our survival.

In fact, collaboration is part of our DNA and is driven by nature, emotions, personal connections, interactions and human evolution.

Collaboration is a law of nature and makes us feel good. It's powered by people through our interactions to produce amazing outcomes.

The remainder of Part 1 will explore the five collaboration DNA themes using over 80 stories collected during the interviews. Over 100 insights will then be shared in Part 2 'How to collaborate' and Part 3 'What is collaboration'.

It's part of our DNA

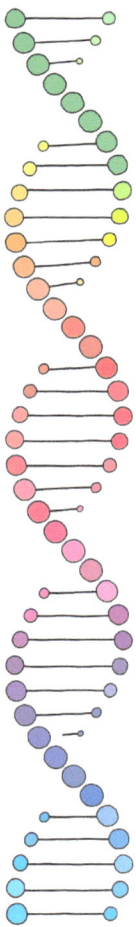

NATURE

EMOTION

CONNECTION

INTERACTION

EVOLUTION

Collaboration is a law of nature and part of our human design, hardwired into our brains and essential to our survival.

Collaboration makes us feel good. It's fed by a growth mindset, self-awareness and connection with our thoughts and emotions.

Collaboration is powered by people who know and harness their 'purpose' to connect, motivate and foster confidence in others.

Collaboration is powered through interactions that are informal and formal and take place virtually, face to face or a hybrid of these.

Collaboration produces ideas and ideas change and evolve humanity because they produce results that are desirable or beneficial.

It's a law of nature

Collaboration is part of our human design, hardwired into our brains and essential to our survival. Its synergy requires less mental and physical effort. The shared responsibility is an investment in the future. Its two-way reciprocal nature builds trust and confidence.

"The desire to collaborate is hardwired into our brains
and DNA; it's deep in our sub-conscious and happens
automatically. Don't fight it; collaboration is how we work."

Professional Musician

It's a law of nature, part of our DNA and wired into our brains

Essentially, collaboration is part of our DNA. We are social beings and collaboration is fundamental to what has brought us to this point in human history.

Social beings

Historian, Yuval Noah Harari explores in his book, 'Sapiens – a brief history of humankind' one possible theory as to why Homo sapiens survived and Neanderthals died out. He explains:

> *Neanderthals typically lived in smaller groups of forty people. In contrast, Homo sapiens' innate social abilities helped them evolve and coexist in much larger groups.*

Our societal groups have grown from hundreds of members to cities of tens of thousands and now, successfully in the most part to 8 billion people spread across the globe. Our inbuilt, natural tendency and programming to collaborate has underpinned this progress.

Part of our human design

We are designed to collaborate and operate as a collective, working together for better outcomes. This allows us to connect, build relationships and feel good. A business improvement manager who has collaborated on many projects believes when collaborating:

Our endorphins are higher, we experience a buzz and a sense of belonging.

Social beings

Collaboration is natural because we all want to feel part of a community. A professional musician believes:

> *This desire is hardwired into our brains deep in our subconscious and happens automatically.*
> *We need to feel loved, have a purpose and regularly interact with others.*
> *Don't fight it; collaboration is how humans are designed to work together.*

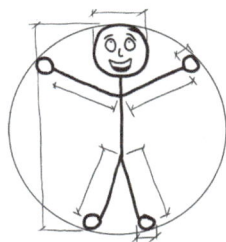

Human design

Essential to survival

A disability advocate with a passion for supporting the rights of people with disabilities believes we are all intimately engaged with each other and need others to survive. He explains:

> *A person with a disability finds it even more important to have a collaborative approach to solving problems. Typically, people don't know how to deal with a person with a disability. They must be treated like any human being.*

Collaboration is essential to survival as a human being.

Human survival

It's a law of nature where synergy and productivity are intertwined

Collaboration is a more efficient use of our human resources, as the combining of skills and perspectives produces better results with less mental and physical effort.

Produces synergy

Synergy is where the interaction of our combined contributions produces something greater than the sum of the individual parts. When we collaborate, one and one are far more than two. Synergy happens everywhere.

An artist reflects on the creative process and synergy:

> *Collaboration in art is honouring the original parts to create something new. For example, if you mix parts A and B to create C, you have made new art. The patterns from A and B have their own benefits and could be similar. However, mixing A and B gives you synergy, a unique pattern C, with new benefits.*

Applying this point of view to ideas, you need to honour and respect people's ideas A and B and use collaboration to move the ideas forward to create a new idea C with benefits people can identify with. Good collaboration is underpinned by synergy; our combined efforts produce more than the sum of our individual contributions.

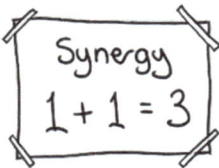

Synergy
$1 + 1 = 3$

Produces synergy

Uses less mental effort

Synergy is productive because we do the same work with less mental effort. An experienced project manager responsible for running multidiscipline projects with experienced experts has observed:

> *Individual specialists use less mental effort when they focus their thinking and contribution on what they know.*

When people work in their comfort zone, it's easy to focus on the task and create good ideas; we feel safe, confident and motivated within our specialty area. When we use combined expertise and skills within a collaboration, it requires less mental effort.

Less mental effort

Uses less physical effort

If we assume a certain amount of work is required to complete a project alone, we use less physical effort when collaborating as the work is divided. Like in every other aspect of life, collaboration is the most efficient way to achieve a goal. A head waiter shares that his Italian restaurant is like a watch with parts, wheels and rotors:

> *When you put them together, they create a machine that tells the time. The restaurant is exactly like that, every single person plays a part and you can't do anything without all the other parts working.*

Synergy is the engine room behind collaboration and is highly productive. It requires less mental and physical effort to get things done and deliver effective outcomes.

Less physical effort

It's a law of nature, an investment in the future and our responsibility

Successful communities and teams
see collaboration as a continuous cycle
of improvement where the ongoing
support and learning are the combined
responsibility of all members.

An investment in the future

Collaboration is an investment in the
future, based on goodwill, where goodwill
is a friendly or helpful attitude towards
each other. Sometime in the future, others
will need your support and you will need
theirs. When you have goodwill, asking for
help is very powerful and is more likely to
be provided. Treat collaboration like a bank
account of goodwill that you can build up
over time and then draw on later.

For example, a senior public servant
working in customs takes a big picture view
explaining:

> *When collaborating, you can
> help someone by allowing them
> to develop, grow and shine. In
> doing so, you are topping up
> your account of goodwill with
> this person.*

Having a friendly or helpful attitude
towards each other means you succeed
together. Underpinning this goodwill is
that collaboration requires discipline and
must be reciprocal. If your behaviours are
genuine and altruistic, others will behave
the same way and the goodwill will flow
back to you.

Investment in
the future

A shared responsibility

An officer in the armed services believes:

> It's about a sense of purpose
> and a shared responsibility for
> bringing your experiences and
> knowledge to the table.

As defence members, they collaborate at
the local, state and international levels.
Typically, their main effort is security and
bringing stability to the situation. However,
underlying this is collaborating with the
locals to bring medical support and restore
critical infrastructure, so people begin to
feel safe, normal and have confidence
in the future. We all have a shared
responsibility to collaborate and invest in
the future.

A shared
responsibility

Pass on knowledge

This responsibility to collaborate and pass
on knowledge is deep within our minds and
soul. As a yoga teacher points out:

> We have seen this throughout
> history as learned people take it
> upon themselves to share what
> they know to make the world
> better.

It's a guru's responsibility to collaborate
with students and pass on knowledge. It's
a manager's responsibility to mentor, a
coach's responsibility to guide and Yoda's
responsibility to help Luke Skywalker
bring balance to the force. Underpinning
this philosophy is that others have learnt
and now it's their time to pass on this
knowledge to the next generation.

Pass on
knowledge

*Its two-way
reciprocal nature
builds trust and
confidence.*

It's a law of nature underpinned by trust, respect, transparency and reciprocation

The best collaboration happens when people feel safe, informed, respected and valued. This mutual trust builds a reciprocal cycle of collaboration.

Built on trust and confidence

In terms of collaboration, trust is a feeling you can rely on a person; you believe they will help and behave in a certain way. They will collaborate sincerely and see it as an investment in their own and other people's long-term future. As a public servant highlights:

> *Collaboration is two-way; people need to trust, have confidence and collaborate with genuine intent.*

Collaboration is fundamental within the public service and occurs across government, agencies and departments. It is underpinned by mutual respect. When collaborating, it is vital at the very end that people walk away with mutual regard, still respecting each other, even if there is disagreement.

As a global business program manager shares:

> *We all know collaboration can sometimes be forced upon us, which tests our levels of respect, trust and confidence. During these times, it's essential to leverage the opportunity by recognising the diversity of the people and respecting everyone's contribution to the collaboration.*

Built on trust and confidence

Collaboration without trust and confidence is likely to be short term and superficial.

Transparent

Collaborating in a transparent and meaningful way invites trust by demonstrating an honest and credible endeavour. As a university lecturer points out:

> *Transparency also improves the likelihood of any outcome being accepted, acted upon and making a positive impact. This acceptance and subsequent ownership leads to a greater commitment to action.*

Collaborating transparently helps to build trust, confidence and respect.

Reciprocal

Collaboration being reciprocal underpins trust, confidence and respect. Simply put, if I help you, you reciprocate and help me. As a sustainability manager highlights:

> *Reciprocal behaviour is critical to successful collaboration. If we have no confidence a person will help us, it's unlikely we will trust them and go out of our way to help them.*

So, for collaboration to be optimised, it must be reciprocal.

Transparent

Reciprocal

Collaboration is about doing things, not owning things, if you are not doing it, it does not happen.

It's a law of nature shown through spirituality

Collaboration is central to all faiths and cultures and is underpinned by relationships with a higher power, oneself, the environment and each other..

Sharing

Collaboration brings a sense of connection to something bigger than ourselves. It's underpinned by a culture of sharing, caring, and respecting. As an indigenous elder points out:

> *As a little kid and young man, we sat in sharing circles and worked things through - we have always worked this way and its part of our culture.*

Collaboration happens when people come together and recognise one person's knowledge is not enough.

Relationships

Collaboration is about the bigger things. The universe is a collaboration. We could not have an earth without Jupiter, earth depends on its relationship with other planets. In fact, earths relationship with the moons gravitational pull creates a climate that makes life possible. As a spiritual leader shares:

> *Relationships are the base of collaboration. Christian faith is about relationships, love and connecting with everyone. Collaboration is building relationships to seek a better world.*

Collaboration happens when we are deeply present with one another; the more deeply we are present, the deeper the collaboration.

Sharing circle

Relationships

Improvement

Collaboration is about working together to improve the world. A recent literature review of verses and words describing collaboration in the Qur'an found four themes:

- equality
- helping each other
- moving towards improvement
- devotion.

When we honour, respect and help each other we successfully improve everyone's lives. As a spiritual leader shares:

> The Qur'an emphasises that collaboration is good work and made possible through teamwork and hope for improvement.

Collaboration moves everyone towards improvement individually and as a society.

Moving towards improvement

Makes us feel good

Successful teams recognise that collaboration is fed by a growth mindset and personal development. It is driven by self-awareness and connection with our thoughts and emotions. It interconnects with all aspects of a person, assisting them to find answers, build resilience, learn new things and feel good.

"When collaborating, our endorphins are higher, we feel happy and experience a bigger buzz and have a sense of belonging."

Business Improvement Manager

Collaboration is fed by a growth mindset and personal development.

Makes us feel good by having a growth mindset and personal development

Collaboration is the merging and moulding of ideas and skills to serve a shared purpose. It requires people to be open to changing and developing their thinking. They see lifelong learning as important to their personal growth.

Having a growth mindset

A growth mindset means you believe that your most basic abilities can be developed through dedication and hard work; brains and talent are just the starting point. In contrast, a fixed mindset means you believe intelligence or talent are simply fixed traits. Central to a growth mindset is lifelong learning and having a beginner's perspective, opening yourself to new ideas by letting go of all preconceived notions.

A growth mindset feeds collaboration, creating new thinking patterns and generating random ideas, leading to different solutions and sustainable success. As Albert Einstein said:

> *"We cannot solve our problems using the same thinking we used to create them."*

Hence, we need to think differently. A growth mindset feeds collaboration as you continually ask questions and reach out to others.

Growth mindset

Shaping our thinking, ideas and vision

Collaboration provides a forum for conversations and allows us to see how our views compare to others. It enables us to reframe our thinking to address other perspectives. A public servant believes:

> *As we collaborate, we undergo a process of reflecting and verbalising thoughts. Some people reflect using internal dialogue and come up with an answer; others arrive at the same point through discussion.*

When collaborating, it's important to verbalise thoughts, allowing others to see your thinking. Collaboration, combined with a growth mindset, provides energy to learn and evolve as we continually develop our thinking.

Highly valued

In the future, personal recognition will be based on how well we collaborate and the ideas we bring to the table. A knowledge worker who uses high-level communication skills and the latest technology to work independently and collaboratively to accomplish complex tasks thinks:

> *Today and into the future, knowledge workers will continue to be measured by their participation, ideas, experiences, interpretations and judgments. The more a knowledge worker collaborates, gets involved and brings diversity of thought to a problem, the more they will be recognised, rewarded and possibly promoted.*

Collaboration is fast becoming a prerequisite for recognition and future personal opportunities.

Shaping our thinking, ideas and vision

Highly valued

Collaboration is driven by self-awareness and connection with our thoughts and emotions.

Makes us feel good by connecting with thoughts, feelings and emotions

The interrelationship between collaboration and our emotions benefits team members individually and collectively and leads to more successful outcomes.

Collaboration improves our emotions and physical and mental wellbeing

An experienced yoga teacher recognises this and shares:

> *Yoga is an old discipline from India that is spiritual and physical. Yoga is essentially a collaboration of activities where 90% is done in silence. It uses breathing techniques, physical exercise and meditation to help improve our physical and mental wellbeing.*

Yoga helps strengthen our emotions by removing inbuilt physical tension from our body, bringing feelings of calm and ease. When a group of people collaborate and do Yoga together, they raise the vibration of the group and everyone's energy in general. For the yoga teacher, the collaboration is successful when people have positive wellbeing, benefiting their mind, body and soul.

Improves our emotions and wellbeing

Feeling and giving love and protection

An experienced project manager who has worked on many projects thinks:

> *Collaboration is feeling and giving love and protection. Underpinning collaboration is our desire to be loved and protected. When collaborating on a project within a successful team, you feel a sense of love and give love. You also feel protected and protective of others, even for people you don't feel a connection with. It may not be the intense feeling of deep affection for your family. All the same, it's still a strong feeling of appreciation and devotion to your team.*

Feeling and giving love and protection

For the project manager, the collaboration is successful when the team feel and give love and protection.

Sharing thoughts, emotions and feelings

The lead cellist from a symphony orchestra believes:

> *Collaborating is sharing thoughts, emotions and feelings through musical language. Playing is like a pipeline. As a collective, an orchestra's thoughts and ideas move down the pipe and are channelled cohesively and played in tune to create a sound. This sound then generates emotions, fear, excitement or calm.*

Thoughts, emotions and feelings

Makes us feel good by being self-aware and connecting with people

Successful collaborators are humble, putting the needs of the group before their own. They understand the power of human connection in motivating individuals and teams.

Connecting with people

Human connection has the power to deepen the moment, inspire change and build trust. A lack of connection or loneliness has been linked to a reduction in physical and mental wellbeing. A national charity takes connecting with people very seriously and shares:

> *Collaboration involves connecting and involving people to be part of our vision.*

They have learned how critical it is to connect, talk and involve their members, volunteers and suppliers. Many of their members are blind, have limited mobility and risk being isolated. By connecting with others, we can lower anxiety and depression, help to regulate our emotions and build higher self-esteem and empathy. Human connection is a powerful human desire and an innate driver for why we collaborate.

Connecting
with people

Being humble and self-aware

Being humble is looking at ourselves objectively and noticing our negative behaviours, such as not admitting mistakes and criticizing others. Then, when we collaborate, we can see how we behave and respond to situations, seeing another person's perspective or taking on positive and negative feedback. An experienced project manager thinks:

> *Being humble provides a new opportunity to learn, reflect and become more self-aware. In a way, it's adopting an altruistic attitude where you are putting the overall team goal ahead of your own needs.*

Being humble and self-aware

A team sport

The Olympic Rhythmic Gymnastics team demonstrates what it is to be humble and self-aware.

> *They believe that as individuals, each gymnast is an elite athlete at the top of their game, but they become Olympians as a group.*

They openly acknowledge that being by themselves, they wouldn't have made it to the Olympics, but collaborating as a group, they did. Even when an individual athlete competes, they have a support team of coaches, training partners, sports psychologists and family.

In truth, when collaborating in sport or life, it's never about just one person and their ideas. The foundation of effective collaboration is being humble, self-aware and knowing it's a team sport and not a solo endeavour.

Team sport

Successful teams find answers and build resilience.

Makes us feel good by finding answers and building resilience

Working together accelerates progress toward superior outcomes as different tasks can be completed simultaneously. Other perspectives and a combined effort help to build resilience and overcome procrastination.

Find the right answers

Collaboration is finding answers to our questions. Because we can't know all the answers as an individual, we need to collaborate and ask people to help. The best part of collaborating is that we can accelerate our individual learning by harnessing the knowledge of others. What could have taken weeks for an individual to solve can now occur in days. Collaboration allows multiple questions to be asked and answered simultaneously, reinforcing that one plus one is more than two when we collaborate.

A team leader within a global company says:

> *It's simple, if you don't know the answer, just ask your network of people; if they don't know the answer, they will ask their network. In a short time, you will find the answer to your question.*

Collaboration brings many minds together to provide solutions to our questions. Finding answers to our questions is integral to collaboration.

Find the right answers

Build resilience

Collaboration builds resilience and enhances our ability to bounce back from difficult life events. Life is in constant change, a fact exacerbated by COVID with its significant disruption to our daily lives. When we collaborate, this improves how we react and manage such changes. We build powerful human connections with each other by collaborating; we don't feel alone; we talk things out and find answers to our questions, reinforcing the proverb, 'a problem shared is a problem halved'.

A small business owner impacted by COVID believes:

> *When we see other perspectives, we feel less overwhelmed, see a future and start making realistic plans to change our situation.*

Overcome procrastination

When we procrastinate, we put off or delay something we must do. It does not go away and often sits in our subconscious mind nagging at us. A university student in her final year shares:

> *It's good to have other people to rely on who push you. Collaborating within a team helps us to overcome procrastination. Others are relying on us and we are accountable; it drives us to do a particular task, even when we don't want to do it, but must.*

When we collaborate, we are accountable to others and get the job done.

Build resilience

Overcome procrastination

Successful teams learn new things and feel good.

Makes us feel good by learning

Successful collaborators enjoy learning and realise that working together provides many opportunities to learn for free.

Programmed into how we learn

Learning is programmed into our brains; we do this without conscious thought or attention. Each day, we take in information and interpret observations, referencing our memories for similar situations or storing away new memories. Acquiring knowledge is not an option; it's linked to our survival. Our ancestors learnt where the best water holes were, what they could safely eat and which animals to avoid. This knowledge was passed on to successive generations. A registered nurse believes:

> *While today's modern world requires different survival skills, the thirst for knowledge remains automatic and programmed into our brains.*

Acquiring more knowledge

Collaborating harnesses this need to acquire knowledge. Over thousands of years, we have learnt sharing knowledge is a good thing. Combining our knowledge has allowed us to solve ongoing problems and given us the confidence to solve future problems. An operations manager running a plant believes:

> *Most people have found that they learn and perform better when others support them. Our personal experience says it's better to work with or consult with people to acquire knowledge to get things done.*

Programmed into how we learn

The idea of collaborating starts when we are young. When a group of seven-year-old students were asked when they last collaborated, their responses included:

> *Playing tag at school, building a hiding place with my sister, figuring out how me and Elsa would stop using Teams chat and say nice things to each other.*

For both young and old, collaborating with others is how we learn.

Learning for free

People have an adventurous spirit, where motivation is a force to conquer new things. Working with and getting to know new people brings diversity, fresh perspectives and insights, which provide new skills. A doctor working in a hospital points out:

> *We learn from others for free when we collaborate. These lessons and experiences stay with us and are placed in our toolbox for the next collaboration.*

When asked to collaborate, take advantage of the free learning.

Acquiring more knowledge

Learning for free

Powered
by people

Collaboration is powered by people
who know and harness their purpose to
motivate and foster confidence in others.
Successful collaborators acknowledge
and facilitate different personalities
and their varying tendencies toward
collaboration. They celebrate diversity of
mind, thought and culture and recognise
the interrelationship between collaboration
and communication.

"It's a beautiful thing for all six of us to be working towards one goal and knowing that without each other we wouldn't be able to do it."

Olympian

Powered by people knowing the WHY and setting goals

Success in collaboration is amplified when there is a clear purpose that is communicated to the group with clear and specific goals.

Knowing and communicating your WHY

Collaboration is knowing your WHY, which inspires you to act. Having a purpose means knowing yourself, your priorities and aligning your behaviours with your desired goal. Establishing your WHY strengthens your confidence and drive, so you feel assertive enough to share and take on others' ideas to improve your thinking. Your WHY also inspires others to act and be part of your collaboration.

Knowing your WHY is part of the equation; the other part is communicating the WHY so people can participate. A member of the armed services who has travelled the world believes:

> *For any given task, it's
> so important the person
> understands WHY they
> are doing it. When people
> understand the WHY, they can
> use their own expertise to solve
> the problem.*

This is the same when a task is part of a collaboration, whether providing medical support, helping a local school, or bringing back infrastructure. Communicating the WHY gives people a sense of purpose and belonging.

Knowing and
communicating
your WHY

Driven by a common purpose

The purpose becomes the engine room and provides the necessary energy and activity to drive collaboration. A senior manager who has led multiple global teams shares:

> *By knowing and communicating the 'WHY' with passion, people will engage with the purpose and feel inspired, finding a way to be involved. To initiate and maintain people's motivation to collaborate, the purpose needs to be sufficiently challenging to keep people inspired and energised but not too unrealistic or difficult that people feel overwhelmed and disconnected.*

If people have a common and challenging purpose, this will provide the essential energy required to collaborate.

Setting common goals

Setting common goals sustains collaboration. Goal definition is critical as it drives motivation and personal satisfaction, triggering genuine collaboration. A team's energy, momentum and intensity are sustained by SMART goals. An experienced executive assistant who has worked for many senior managers believes:

> *While collaborating, we are always aiming to reach an end goal, working with subject matter experts to tap into their ideas. Part of this process is negotiating an outcome to progress your thinking and persuading others to be aligned with your outcome, so it becomes theirs.*

Having a common end goal to work towards helps to direct and motivate people when collaborating.

Driven by a
common purpose

Setting
common goals

Powered by people's motivation and confidence

People intrinsically want to be part of something bigger as it gives purpose and meaning, inspiring confidence and motivating us to achieve goals. This ongoing interaction builds and sustains momentum, which keeps people motivated.

Motivation

Purpose drives motivation, motivation drives collaboration and collaboration achieves our goals.

A planning engineer working remotely at home realised:

> *Collaborating during lockdown has resulted in less face-to-face interaction. Most of the work is now done remotely via email or Zoom. The challenge we faced was how to work as a team when we couldn't interact. We learnt the secret is not to focus on collaboration itself. The focus needs to be on how we motivate people then collaboration will happen. We found if people are motivated, they will find innovative, fun and productive ways to interact.*

It's a lack of motivation that stops collaboration, not remote work. Motivation propels people to collaborate towards a common goal.

Motivation

Momentum

Successful collaboration is a positive force
which helps a team to build momentum.
A team leader working in the energy
industry thinks:

> *Collaboration becomes the*
> *glue holding people together in*
> *pursuit of a common purpose*
> *providing people with a*
> *reason to act, motivating us to*
> *collaborate which in turn creates*
> *momentum to sustain the team.*

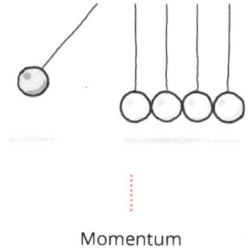

Momentum

Confidence

People's confidence in themselves and each
other powers collaboration. Confidence is
feeling sure of yourself and your abilities.
Collaboration requires people to put
themselves out there and be exposed to
feeling vulnerable.

David Kelly, co-founder of the design firm
IDEO, talks at length about building your
confidence in his book, 'Creative confidence
- Unleashing The Creative Potential Within
Us'. He says:

> *"At its core, creative confidence is*
> *your ability to create change in the*
> *world around you. It's the conviction*
> *that you can achieve what you set*
> *out to do and this self-assurance,*
> *this belief in your creative capacity,*
> *lies at the heart of innovation".*

Confidence

Bringing creative confidence to any
collaboration will have a profound impact.
If you believe you can change the world,
you are more likely to succeed. People will
be inspired by your conviction and want
to collaborate. Collaborating with creative
confidence leads to innovation and positive
change.

*Acknowledge
and facilitate
different
personalities
and their varying
tendencies
toward
collaboration.*

Powered by people's personalities and tendency to collaborate

Successful collaborators acknowledge and facilitate different personalities such as introverts and extroverts. They also know their team and are sensitive to their personal and professional demands.

Personalities - introverts

People's personalities influence collaboration. People may identify themselves as having an extroverted or introverted personality. Extroverts develop ideas by talking and verbalising their thoughts, typically thriving in dynamic, physical face-to-face social environments. In contrast, introverts develop ideas through reflection, thoughts and feelings. Frequently, they are more selective and thrive in calm environments, preferring solitude. A team leader notes:

> *The recent shift to remote collaboration has suited introverts who have found their voice and confidence to share ideas.*

Personalities - extroverts

By contrast, extroverts have struggled, unable to talk and gain energy from the group. It's quite conceivable that they may feel isolated, uninspired and left out. People's personality traits can have a significant influence on collaboration.

Introverts

A performance poet reflected on how personalities can affect our work and explained:

> *I am on different occasions either an introvert and extrovert. I must be an introvert to write the work. Even when collaborating, I don't usually write in the same room as other people; that's my introvert trait as a writer. Then I must memorise the poem, jump on stage and be an extrovert to present it to the world with confidence and a commanding presence.*

Extroverts

Collaboration supports both the introvert and extrovert traits.

Identifying and managing levels of involvement

Recognising people's tendency to collaborate is important. We all want to collaborate as part of our DNA, but some are more predisposed than others. Good collaboration is identifying and managing people's levels of involvement. By nature, we are social creatures, and some of us, can be offended when not involved. Speaking with one person and not another can make a person feel left out. At best, this person could simply disconnect and disengage; at worst, they could actively de-rail the collaboration.

A strategic planner working in the minerals industry thinks:

> *Some people may genuinely want to collaborate; however, they are overwhelmed with existing commitments. In this case, it is helpful to involve them only when necessary while keeping them up to date with ongoing communications.*

Identifying and managing levels of involvement

Sometimes, people's tendency to collaborate is driven by their day-to-day circumstances, family commitments, feeling poorly, or having a bad day.

Powered by people's diversity of mindset, thought and culture

Successful collaborators celebrate diversity of beliefs and distinctive views, challenge traditional thought patterns and paradigms and embrace multicultural perspectives.

Diverse mindsets

Diverse mindsets power collaboration. Your mindset is a set of beliefs that shape how you make sense of the world and yourself. It influences how you think, feel and behave in any given situation. When we collaborate with others, we all bring different mindsets and distinctive perspectives on a situation or problem. It's as if we are looking at the same problem from different angles and each of us is seeing different aspects, nuances and symptoms of the problem. As a result, we can make connections between different ideas and build new insights based on a deeper understanding of the problem.

A disability advocate, reinforcing the importance of diverse perspectives, shares:

> *We all bring attributes to society. We miss unique perspectives by not including people with disabilities in our collaboration.*

Engaging people with a disability is important to help us make new connections by seeing life through a different lens.

Diverse thinking powers collaboration. It focuses on breaking down traditional thought patterns to find new paths to ideas. It emphasises the 'movement value' of ideas – allowing people with different mindsets to collaborate and take a known idea somewhere else and create new ideas.

Diverse mindsets

Diverse thinking

A senior manager leading teams that study creative options believes:

> *Diverse thinking can also be challenging as it takes people out of their comfort zone. However when we provide a safe space without criticism, people feel empowered to engage in divergent thinking.*

Diverse thinking takes a concerted effort as people must be open to uncharted pathways.

Diverse cultures

Culture brings wide and varied mindsets, introducing perspectives that make collaboration meaningful, inspiring and productive. These different perspectives bring passion, new thought, diverse thinking and amazing outcomes. An operation manager from the waste industries shares:

> *Our workforce includes six different cultures. Many have recently come from countries at war, having spent time in refugee camps. They just want to have a seat at the table and do the right thing. With their unique background, personality, life experiences and beliefs, they bring a genuine passion for collaborating and working together.*

Diverse cultures bring a depth of thinking and perspectives to any collaboration.

Diverse thinking

Diverse cultures

Recognise the interrelationship between collaboration and communication.

Powered by people's communication

Collaboration is powered by clear, specific and timely communication in all its forms. Collaboration is powered by people communicating to share or exchange information and knowledge. Communication is designed to build awareness, create interest, motivate people and organise resources. We communicate verbally and non-verbally and use written communication in words and images to help people understand the information. Finally, effective communication is listening and showing you are paying attention and are genuinely interested and getting value. It's respecting the communication in a polite and constructive manner, whether you agree or disagree.

Clear

A nursing manager has an interesting perspective on the critical relationship between collaboration and clear communication.

Clear communications

> *In a hospital, patient and staff safety is paramount. We could not do our job and achieve the outcomes without collaboration. Any report or near-miss comes back to poor collaboration and possible miscommunication. For example, if we are 15 minutes late for theatre, we put in a risk report to understand what happened so we can learn from the situation. It's critical to know why. Was the communication problem verbal or nonverbal, written or visual, or are people not listening?*

Collaboration and communication are intrinsically linked.

Specific

The airline industry is underpinned by effective collaboration and communication. An airline pilot shares:

Specific communications

> *Communication is key; the flow of specific information provides a shared understanding to the staff and passengers. Airlines are very procedural, ensuring boarding, check-in, food and flying happen safely. Collaboration and communication are critical as no two flights are the same. Some flights have rules for unaccompanied children: they must sit at the back of the plane and be chaperoned. Other flights may have disabled passengers requiring specific support.*

Timely

The relationship between collaboration and communication can be seen when a performance poet and symphony orchestra perform for 500 people.

> *The performance is a combination of many forms of communication, timed to work together to enhance the message. The poet uses his original words to verbally communicate, using tone and rhythm to further express his message. The orchestra's performance provides further meaning. Everyone must listen and play their part at just the right time, combining to communicate much more than the original words.*

Timely communications

The way we communicate can have a profound impact on collaboration.

Through interactions

Collaboration is powered through interactions that vary in their context and makeup. Formal interactions make use of well-defined processes, while informal interactions happen more casually. The context may be narrow within your immediate network or broad involving industry wide or cross industry contributors. It may take place virtually, face to face or a hybrid of these. Finally, it may be an evolving interaction driven by disruption, advancing technology or changing social expectations.

"When the pendulum swings back from fully remote, it will not be only face-to-face. It will be in the middle and 'hybrid'."

Global Manager

Collaboration is powered through interactions that vary in their context and makeup, and that make use of well-defined processes and informal interactions.

Through interactions that are formal and informal

Collaboration is people coming together and interacting for a common purpose. This desire to interact is ingrained in our DNA. Interacting makes us feel good as we connect with others and our emotions. It enables us to find answers, build resilience and learn. When interacting, collaboration can be both formal and informal.

Formal and informal interactions

Formal interactions are explicit and precise. They are typically well-defined processes describing how, when and where the interactions will happen. An experienced musician believes:

> *Some collaborations require a dedicated formal space where musicians can work. Producers often hire a studio where people are locked away uninterrupted to collaborate from start to finish on an album.*

Formal interaction

Formal interactions provide a specific time and space for people to collaborate.

Informal interactions are less structured; they can be intimate, relaxed and spontaneous. A General Practitioner working within a medical practice sees informal corridor consultations as extremely valuable:

> *It's when doctors ask questions between patient appointments as they pass each other in a corridor—seeking a new perspective or reassurance on a patient's diagnosis.*

Informal interaction

In business, this is often called the water cooler chat. Informal interactions are a daily occurrence as people casually collaborate.

Combination

Typically, collaboration is a combination of both interactions and can appear seamless. A nursing manager in a major hospital sees collaboration as a blend of formal and informal:

> We complete a formal handover meeting at 6:30 a.m., 1 p.m. and 7 p.m. to discuss the day and any problems. Whereas throughout the day, we informally capture patient feedback, speak on the phone and work with surgeons in the operating room.

The best collaboration is a blend of formal and informal interactions.

Combination

A culture of collaboration

A culture of collaboration underpins formal and informal interactions where people see the big picture and engage in the collaboration purpose. A public servant who leads a department and collaborates with other agencies thinks:

> My work focuses on the culture by identifying and systematically removing barriers to effective collaboration. We schedule formal meetings to force collaboration and strive to make people feel safe when collaborating informally.

Collaboration is best when underpinned by a culture of open communication and engagement.

Culture
of collaboration

Through narrow interactions

When interacting, collaboration can be narrow within your immediate network of people and circle of influence, where the scope is limited. This type of interaction can be dynamic and compelling, requiring energy and urgency. It can also be lively and bustling as people get things done. In contrast, it can be uncertain and constantly changing. Collaboration is always changing; it can be dynamic, compelling, lively and uncertain.

Dynamic

When collaborating, interactions can be dynamic. As the lead cellist for a symphony orchestra shares:

> *Collaboration within the music world needs to be dynamic and energetic; you need to be fast, adaptable and react to the moment. As musicians, it's in our DNA, an unspoken thing. Every day the conductor and repertoire could be different. We could be doing an opera or concert. As one performance ends, we start another. It is an instant rolling collaboration exercise. Improvisation happens consistently.*

Collaboration can be dynamic, forcing you to be agile, diligent and engaged.

Dynamic

Compelling

When collaborating, interactions can be compelling. A pilot shares:

Compelling

> When flying a plane at 36000 feet, interactions between the cabin crew are compelling and require immediate attention. When solving problems on an aircraft, the pressure and stress can be intense. When flying, you have a finite time window. You can set yourself up for failure by rushing; if you have three minutes, take every second to decide.

Airlines do lots of simulator training to model these scenarios. Collaboration can be compelling; it's crucial the right decisions are made in a timely manner.

Uncertain

When collaborating, interactions can be uncertain. Policemen and women working on the front line dealing with people's emotions recognise that interactions can be uncertain and risky.

> Within the police force, crises can frequently escalate and worsen (for example, domestic and family violence). In these situations, the outcome of any collaboration and interaction can be unclear and precarious. Because of this, we must constantly collaborate broadly, engaging with the individuals, communities, other agencies and Non-Government Organisations (NGOs) to understand how everyone can contribute to the solutions.

Uncertain

Collaboration can be uncertain as people's emotions are involved, making the outcomes risky and unclear.

*The context
may be broad,
involving
industry wide or
cross industry
contributors.*

Through broad interactions

Collaboration is people coming together
and interacting. It can be narrow within
your immediate network of people,
or broad with people outside your
department, such as external partners,
governments, industries and countries.

Internal and external partners

Collaborating broadly involves interacting
with internal and external partners. An
experienced public servant has recently
seen a shift to a much broader interaction:

> *Our collaboration now extends
> outside our department
> to other jurisdictions and
> government agency networks.
> This allows us to learn from
> each other and work together
> to benchmark, identify best
> practice and adapt others'
> novel ideas for our purpose.
> For example, we collaborated
> with the Health Department to
> design a COVID safe election
> in a society where voting is
> compulsory.*

Collaborating externally to our department
opens new ways for us all to improve.

Within and across industries

Collaborating within similar industries
provides opportunities to leverage off
shared experiences. The ongoing transition
to building a sustainable world has a
significant impact on existing industries and
creating new industries.

INTERNAL / EXTERNAL

Internal and
external partners

It will require collaboration on a global scale driven by people's desire to make the world a better place, along with economics and changes in regulations.

An experienced surveyor working within the international maritime industry has seen a recent push for more collaboration and thinks:

> Traditionally, it's a slow-paced industry without a disrupter to drive innovation and collaboration. The environment has become a big issue and long-term predictions for shipping suggest that it will move to a more land-based supply chain. The big heavy stuff will remain on ships that will slow down to burn less fuel. The smaller, more urgent items will go via air or road. There are now industry forums for ship owners to collaborate and address this significant issue.

Collaborating across the maritime industry can accelerate their shift to becoming a sustainable and responsible industry.

Globally

The use of virtual technology has made global collaboration easy. It has opened our horizons; people are just an email or zoom call away. We have access to experts regardless of their geographical location. It enables us to share resources and ideas as we learn together. A meteorologist with a passion for the weather shared:

> We collaborate with other countries forecasting tropical cyclones to know what best practice is and what does and does not work.

With the use of the internet, collaborating globally is at your fingertips.

Within and across industries

Globally

It may take place virtually, face to face or a hybrid of these.

Through blended interactions

Effective collaboration is likely to be a blended approach of virtual, hybrid and face-to-face interactions. Traditionally, face-to-face was the most common form of collaboration. However, with the onset of COVID, the world moved to fully remote collaborative meetings. As COVID tapers off, businesses expect to conduct more hybrid collaboration meetings involving a face-to-face team and remote participants. A commercial manager within a global company thinks:

> *Over time, face-to-face may even become a luxury, as technology is guiding us to remote options.*

Effective collaboration is likely to be a blended approach depending on the collaboration scope and who will be involved.

Remote

Some industries and jobs flourish with remote interactions, although they can come with challenges. For example, a global manager who spends all day processing and analysing data reflected:

> *Working remotely has proved very flexible and effective, although it raised some critical issues, including digital fatigue, working long hours and a blurred work-life balance.*

(Attending 34 hours of MS Teams meetings a week, 100 emails and 80 What's App messages a day while working on the dinner table with your camera on with your family in the background takes its toll.)

Remote

Your job will drive the types of collaboration interactions; managing the intrusive nature of remote work will be the challenge.

Hybrid

Hybrid collaboration will become common as people move back to the office while others dial in to collaborate. A human resource manager feels that hybrid meetings introduce an imbalance of power between the people in the room and remote participants:

> *People in the room speak more and often have side conversations. The remote people can disconnect and feel like second class citizens. We have learnt to focus on remote people to ensure all participants can equally contribute to hybrid collaborations.*

Hybrid collaboration is becoming more common and requires a deliberate effort to ensure all participants are equally engaged.

Face to face

Face to face collaboration will continue to be a preferred option for some industries. A secondary school teacher who works with disadvantaged children believes:

> *Secondary education will be face-to-face. Teachers continually react to the room's dynamics and working virtually causes significant problems. Students don't necessarily follow the rules.*

Collaborating face to face is the preferred approach for some industries and jobs such as education and entertainment.

Hybrid

Face to face

*It may be
an evolving
interaction
driven by
disruption,
advancing
technology or
changing social
expectations.*

Through evolving interactions

Collaboration will continue to evolve as people's expectations and technology evolve. Historically we collaborated face to face or by mail. Technology advanced and collaboration shifted to telephones and emails and now the internet using Zoom and digital tools. The future of collaboration will be different. Virtual reality will superimpose people into virtual spaces where they collaborate and solve problems. People will collaborate with computers, systems and robots. One thing we can be sure of is that how we interact will continue to evolve and change.

Disruption

Collaboration can be driven by disruption. The onset of COVID brought significant and lasting changes to how we interact, live and work. The emphasis on virtual interaction has grown dramatically as people connect via the internet. What seemed distant technology is now standard and products like 'zoom' have entered our language and lifestyle, opening us to try new things. As a long-term public servant who has seen many changes noted:

> *The COVID crisis forced people to look for new ways of working and reaching out for help. Traditional arguments about demarcation and whose job it is are less critical.*

Disruption

The crisis has opened a new virtual collaboration space for people to communicate. We can be sure that collaboration interactions will continue to evolve and change as people transition to a virtual world.

Changing expectations

People's changing expectations will drive collaboration. An actor working in live theatre believes:

> There will be more collaboration in the future, reflecting how people's expectations continue to evolve. People want to hear different voices, voices of colour and diversity and more female voices.

It will no longer be just following the script. The actors and everyone involved will bring their own experience into a performance. Collaboration interactions will continue to change, reflecting people's new expectations.

Technological advancement

Collaboration will be driven by technological development. Collaboration between people and technology will continue to evolve and expand. A mathematician observed and reflected on the role of technology in the future and believes:

> We may skip people altogether and use self-teaching algorithms to generate ideas. Expert systems will see the data and then provide solutions.

People's roles will change as machines collaborate. Collaboration into the future will continue to be driven by big data and technology.

Changing expectations

Technological advancement

Produces outcomes

Collaboration produces ideas and ideas change the world. Interacting with a focus on a common purpose produces alignment and clarity. Working together in a committed way provides a mechanism or routine to build relationships and a community over time. These connections and the common purpose produce engagement and then commitment. Collaboration is part of human nature because it produces results that are desirable or beneficial.

"What you bring to the collaboration
is not what you say or do, but rather the energy
you bring to uplift people."

Yoga teacher

Produces ideas

Collaboration produces ideas and ideas change the world. Ideas lead to creativity and innovation, replacing something existing with something new. Ideas illustrate our thinking and enable people to communicate their understanding, insights or perceptions and build alignment. When people collaborate, the number, speed and quality of ideas increase. Collaboration drives ideation and improvement to broaden people's views and foster shared accountability. Ideas change the world, but collaboration makes it happen.

Drives ideation and improvement

Collaboration propels ideation and improvement in the process of collecting, collating and choosing ideas. Collecting is an open, divergent process, brainstorming as many ideas as possible. Collating is a convergent process to remove clutter and sharpen people's thinking. Choosing filters high potential ideas with which to progress. An operations manager who has worked as an ex-pat across the world and now leads a global improvement program believes:

> *The group will always beat the lone genius. Brainstorming is designed to have people spark off each other and continue to move the idea forward.*

Collaboration drives ideation and improvement.

Drives ideation and improvement

Broadens people's views

Collaboration broadens people's views by enabling them to see other perspectives and new ideas. A general manager focused on technical work and business improvement believes that:

> *Collaboration allows us to reach out to others to improve a concept or process, which is essential to help clarify thinking and build confidence in our thoughts. Someone else has the expertise we do not have. Collaborating with others drives innovation and extends ideas by allowing us to diverge and then converge our multiple perspectives.*

The more perspectives there are, the better the insights, the more ideas.

Broadens
people's views

Builds shared ownership and accountability

Finally, collaboration builds shared ownership and accountability for ideas. Implementing an idea requires people to take ownership and be accountable for the subsequent change. Ownership and accountability for ideas is one way to measure people's value. A knowledge worker who spends most of her day collaborating on Zoom reflects:

> *In a digital world, many workers are not necessarily delivering products in person. We sit in the background, where value is measured in our ideas and productivity. Recognition in the future will be based on how well we collaborate and the ideas we bring to the table.*

Shared ownership and accountability for ideas can change the world.

Builds shared ownership
and accountability

*Interacting
with a focus
on a common
purpose
produces
alignment and
clarity.*

Produces alignment

Alignment is a state of agreement among people who have a common cause or viewpoint. Building alignment takes several conversations and regular collaboration to improve people's clarity and erase uncertainty and confusion. Having common understanding and goals enables people to sing off the same song sheet, making the road smoother. Collaboration produces alignment, clarity and focus on a common purpose.

Singing off the same song sheet

When people agree and are aligned with a common understanding, they are of one mind, in tune and playing on the same team. A multicultural recycling factory manager, passionate about building an inclusive and aligned team, want people to sing off the same song sheet:

> *Every morning we have a
> 30-minute session with staff
> and then with each shift. It is
> a deliberate focus to stop and
> collaborate to get the same
> messages across.*

This is time well spent to ensure everyone has a voice, up and down and across the factory. Collaboration ensures people are in sync and singing off the same song sheet.

Singing off the same
song sheet

Shared understanding of problems

Collaboration builds a shared understanding of problems. Problems take on many forms; they can be dilemmas requiring a choice between two equally undesirable events, obstacles to be overcome, or questions to be considered. Collaboration brings different perspectives, insights and understanding. A senior engineer leading many cross-functional teams concludes:

Shared understanding of problems

> To understand a problem, you need to share information, ask people their thoughts and collect different opinions. Capturing this in a problem definition statement creates alignment and produces better solutions.

Collaboration builds a shared understanding of problems.

Making the road smoother

Managing deadlines and people's personalities can be challenging, creating bumps in the road. Collaboration fosters involvement and ownership, leading people to discuss and endorse your work, smoothing the road ahead. An experienced manager who has led many teams recognises the importance of collaborating:

> We must collaborate, so people feel involved. It can sometimes be a political exercise; however, we know that not collaborating will cause further stress down the track since people want to be heard.

Making the road smoother

Collaboration builds a sense of involvement, making the road a lot smoother.

Working together in a committed way provides a mechanism or routine to build relationships and a community over time.

Produces connections

Collaboration produces connections by creating a space to foster affinity, trustful relationships and community, and act as one. The act of collaborating provides a mechanism or routine to build relationships and a community over time.

Community

Collaboration builds a community by fostering growth and connections as people work as one. The more collaboration, the deeper the connections. The CEO of a regional recycling factory believes collaboration underpins their success:

> *The quarterly barbeque is symbolic and builds a sense of community. For many, it is the most important event in the year, thanking us personally for our efforts. As the CEO cooking the BBQ, it is amazing when people thank you. We always celebrate with food; the smells bring the community together. By creating a community, we have also built a village where 65% of our team have more than ten years' service in a dirty and smelly job. Through our community, we change the lives of our teams and their families. We try hard to integrate people into our community – maybe that is why they stay so long.*

Collaboration builds a community that can grow into a village.

Community

Affinity

Collaboration nurtures our affinity by showing how similar we are. These similarities build trust and connection. A creative artist and musician who has spent years looking for similarities believes:

> We bring similar things together when we collaborate. We come from the same root, even if we live in different places. My art was 100% Iranian and now I see the similarities between calligraphy and indigenous art. My art is now 50% inspired by nature and aboriginal art.

Demonstrating our similarities and common ground makes it possible to build affinity and connections.

Affinity

Trust

Collaboration and relationships are underpinned by trust. Trust is having a firm belief in a person's reliability, honesty and ability so you can be confident as the relationship develops. A senior policeman who has travelled and worked in diverse roles has learnt:

> Collaboration is not achieved through a power base of authority. The police uniform helps with the initial introduction and credibility, although it is not the dominant driver of collaboration. Trust needs to be at the forefront of people's thinking if a relationship is to develop. If people have a trusting relationship, there is a level of understanding, commitment and respect.

Trust is central to relationships and people connecting.

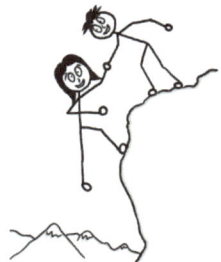

Trust

These connections and the common purpose produce engagement and then commitment.

Produces engagement

Collaboration produces engagement and then commitment. When people collaborate, we create a space where people can come together, connect and engage. The more engaged people are, the more present, aware, mindful and conscious they are. This leads to a shared commitment to each other and their work. They openly communicate, look for and share ways to improve, see the big picture and take a collaborative outlook. Collaboration has the power to engage people and secure their commitment.

Engaged and motivated

Collaboration makes people more engaged and motivated. When we are motivated, we feel an urge to get things done; it's our internal drive to keep moving forward and act towards a goal. Our passion and enthusiasm become contagious and start to motivate others. A senior study manager who has experienced the transition to a virtual world has observed:

> *People progress less when in isolation due to the lack of interaction. Working from home for extended periods can be draining. Collaborating as a team helps us interact and this engagement helps increase people's energy and motivation.*

Collaboration keeps people engaged, motivated and energised.

Engaged
and motivated

Commitment

Collaboration is an informal type of stakeholder engagement influencing the success of your work. A strategy portfolio manager with many years of experience engaging with stakeholders shares:

> *Our desired outcome is to have stakeholders engaged and supporting the work. Collaboration helps us understand each other's perspectives and knowledge. By listening to people's concerns, we can develop ways to maintain their commitment to the project.*

Collaboration is an informal way to understand stakeholders' concerns and needs.

Connections

Collaboration is a shared and connected experience driven by engagement. When we collaborate, we have shared experiences and memories that connect us. An experienced and highly successful global manager believe:

> *Successful teams collaborate and most people want to be part of a successful team. We often talk about a successful project and reflect on our journey. We remember how we engaged, celebrated and overcame barriers. These memories describe a shared experience as the committed team adapted and changed along the way.*

Collaboration provides the platform to collect our shared experiences and memories and connect us long after the collaboration stops.

Project commitment

Connections

Collaboration is part of human nature because it produces results that are desirable or beneficial.

Produces results

Collaboration produces results that are desirable and beneficial. This may be something we can touch, like a new report or way of working, or less obvious, like building a team spirit and a sense of belonging. Desirable results are beautiful and bring pleasure, while beneficial results are advantageous and add value. Collaboration can produce many tangible and intangible results that are desirable or beneficial.

Results are beautiful and make sense

An Iranian refugee to Australia who spent time in immigration detention has shared his skill as an artist combining calligraphy and nature to create images. He believes everyone can understand Art:

> *During my exhibition of paintings bringing plants and calligraphy together, one visitor exclaimed what a beautiful plant, another person noted what delicate calligraphy. In art, this is a successful collaboration as the work made sense to them and they could see the plant or calligraphy and connect to the artwork.*

The best collaborations are beautiful, bring pleasure and make sense – people simply connect with them.

Results are beautiful and make sense

Results improve how we manage change within our lives

An experienced engineer who made a midlife change to teaching high school mathematics believes things are changing all the time:

> *Life is constant change. Our reaction to those changes can be improved by collaborating and sharing. Human beings are social beings; the evolution of our species has pushed us to be more social. To work and survive in a changing world, we need to consistently collaborate with others to engage and manage life's changes.*

Collaboration is positive as it improves how we react and manage change within our lives.

Results are helpful and constructive

A member of the armed services who has served in multiple campaigns around the world describes the results of collaboration:

> *During an operation, we collaborate with the police force, border control, local populations and medical centres. The main driving force is to help make life easier. For example, during an operation, we carry out basic first aid on less critical injuries, helping to free up the medical system for people with serious injuries. At a sub-conscious level, we give people the confidence to do their job by being both physically and morally supported.*

Collaboration is worthwhile; it helps people, making their life easier and less troubled.

Results improve how we manage change within our lives

Results are helpful and constructive

It's part of our DNA

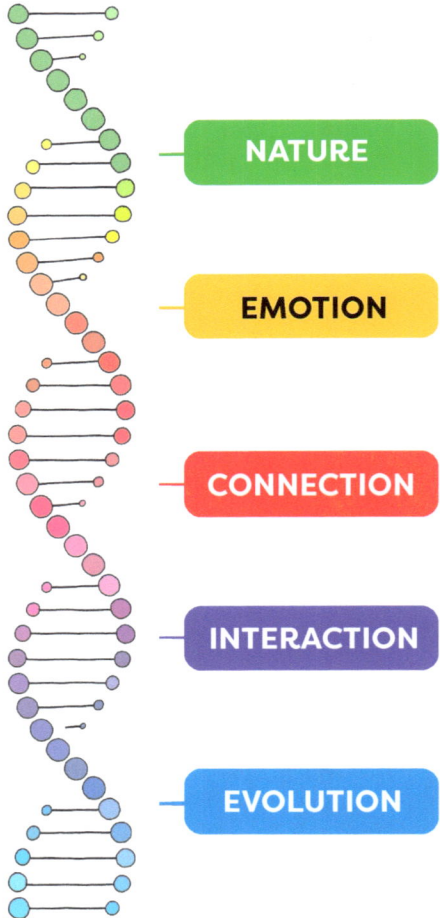

Collaboration is part of our human design, fed by a growth mindset and personal development.

It is powered by people who know and harness their purpose to motivate and foster confidence in others through interactions that vary in their context and makeup.

Collaboration produces ideas, and ideas change the world.

NATURE

EMOTION

CONNECTION

INTERACTION

EVOLUTION

Reflection

What is your collaboration story?

Write down your thoughts about when you have identified with these concepts when collaborating.

*"As individuals
we make
sound, when we
collaborate, we
make music."*

**Professional
Musician**

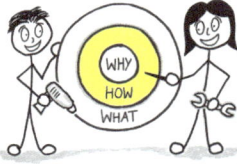

Part 2 -
How to
collaborate

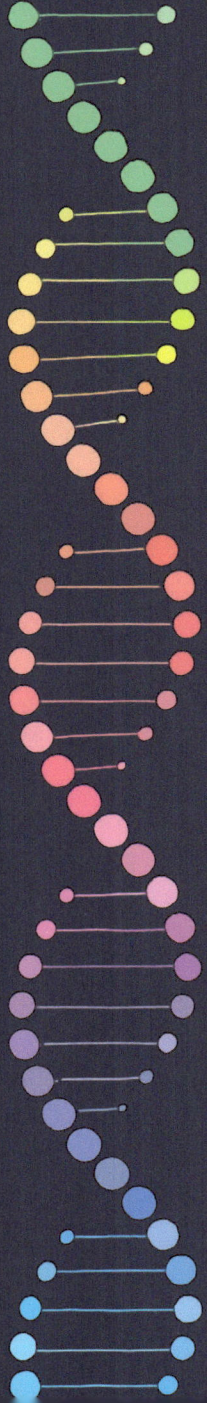

"Over time, face-to-face may even become a luxury."

Resource Strategist

Collaboration in a digital world

The future of collaboration will be digital. We will use our digital devices to communicate and interact to produce ideas, alignment, connections, engagement and results. Digital collaboration is not new; we have been using emails and mobile phones for years to communicate and interact.

However, COVID has introduced a new era of collaboration where we have shifted to the online world. We now interact seamlessly across the globe using online meeting platforms like 'Zoom', digital whiteboards like 'Miro' and team chatrooms like 'What's app'.

Work is completed synchronously online, in real-time, regardless of your location and time zone. Alternatively, work is completed asynchronously using shared documents around the clock, independently of each other.

The younger generations embrace digital collaboration as they feel comfortable with the technology. In contrast, older generations may struggle with the change, have bad experiences and cling to working face to face which is ingrained in how they work.

The new era of collaboration is not without its challenges. It comes with both rewards and threats. For example, how do you embrace the enormous benefits of a digital approach while not losing the social connections of face to face?

The good news is that it's not that difficult; we simply require a slightly different approach underpinned by some new skills and digital tools. It's looking at collaboration as a campaign of short, focused interactions spaced over several weeks.

This collaboration campaign approach helps to manage and guide collaborators over time and across varied platforms while maintaining transparency, engagement and a common purpose.

"Alone we are elite athletes, as a group we are Olympians."

Olympic Gymnast

Collaboration campaign

A collaboration campaign is a strategic set of activities over time guiding, engaging and motivating people with a shared purpose to develop and achieve outcomes while maintaining transparency, alignment and common goals.

Why use this approach?

If we think collaboration is about one interaction, we have it wrong. A meeting is simply part of a bigger game to improve and change how we work. Effective collaboration happens when one interaction simply leads to another interaction and then another and when viewed from a distance, this series of interactions looks like a collaboration campaign.

The benefits of adopting a collaboration campaign approach are that it:

- Takes people on a journey of awareness, understanding and adoption to build alignment, clarity and focus.
- Increases levels of commitment by informing and educating over time to form a foundation for people to commit.
- Is easier to arrange and access people for short, sharp and focused interactions as opposed to one long meeting.
- Allows incubation time between interactions so our subconscious brain can continue to work and create new insights, ideas and clarity on the problem.
- Involves regular communications to connect people and share information to build a deeper understanding of issues.

"Following the pandemic, a new set of collaboration tools have emerged and our expectations towards live, in-person, events have changed. We now realise that reuniting a team from all around the world should be treated as a privilege and that we must extract maximum value from it for it to be sustainable, to the environment and to our business. To achieve that, our team have moved toward a collaboration campaign that started months before the event and continued months after.

During the campaign, team members got to know each other, presented their site, shared their realities and the challenge they face every day. And they did all that virtually. When they met in person, it was just like old friends getting together after a long time; we all hit the ground running. We also realised that even more preparation could have been done before the live event and this is something we will implement in the future. Now that we have collaborated using this hybrid approach, no one wants to go back to the old methods."

Asset Management Lead

Collaboration
campaign in action

Collaboration types

Traditionally, face-to-face was the most common form of collaborative interaction. With the onset of COVID the world moved to fully remote collaboration interactions.

Without a mandated reason to avoid face to face collaboration, we are free to choose according to the needs of the campaign, including a blend of collaboration models.

Virtual collaboration has no central location and everyone is 100% remote.

Hybrid collaboration involves a face-to-face team collaborating with remote participants.

Face-to-face collaboration located in one location.

What does 'good' look like?

We have all attended face to face meetings or workshops where people come together to interact and collaborate towards a common goal. Technology has changed how we interact by moving collaboration into a virtual world. Digital whiteboards, MS teams and Zoom mean we can be remote from each other and also produce ideas, build alignment, make connections and deliver results.

Collaborating in a digital world is a little harder to visualise. In principle, it's like interacting face to face, although centred on our computer screens. The screen has become a window to a virtual and global world where we engage and solve problems remotely. People share screens, turn on their camera and interact on digital whiteboards in real-time.

The following pages paint a picture of what good collaboration looks like. It describes virtual, hybrid and face-to-face collaboration in terms of operating in a digital world. It shows how work is done, the levels of productivity, how people feel, numbers of participants and typical duration.

Simply review the collaboration types and use your imagination to picture digital collaboration. Reflect on each type and envisage how you would use them in your day-to-day interactions.

What 'good' looks like

Virtual collaboration

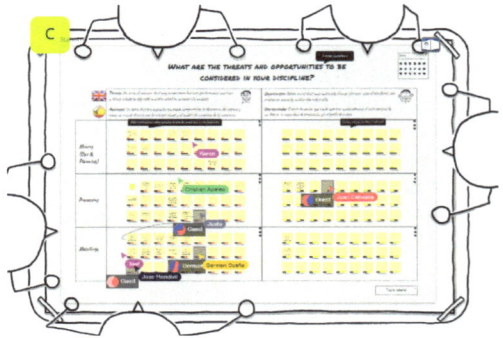

What you will see:

- Most work is done in silence on a digital whiteboard.
- Conversations encouraged in breakout groups.
- Excellent productivity, 20 people, 200 ideas in 30 minutes.
- Group feedback directed through structured share out sessions.
- Introverts empowered as their ideas are captured - extroverts struggle.
- Ideas exported directly off the digital whiteboard into Excel.
- Up to 100 participants.
- Typical duration from 30 minutes to 2 hours.
- Multiple facilitators behind the scenes on the digital whiteboard.
- Significant planning to ensure scope and technology are delivered successfully.

People working remotely

Hybrid collaboration

What you will see:

- People in the room face-to-face and people working remotely via Zoom.
- All participants working on a digital whiteboard.
- Remote people given equal importance by the facilitator.
- Ideas exported directly off the digital whiteboard into Excel.
- Typical duration from 30 minutes to 2 hours to ensure remote people remain engaged.
- Five people face-to-face and five virtual participants to balance influence.
- Multiple facilitators behind the scenes on the digital whiteboard.
- Significant planning to ensure scope and technology are delivered successfully.

Pictured: Five people using the digital whiteboard on their computers, with three people on the same whiteboard via remote.

People in the same room and others remote

"We collaborate so we can learn from other people."

Primary School Student

Face-to-face collaboration

What you will see:

- Most work done verbally as people collaborate and discuss ideas.
- Conversations building lasting relationships.
- Productivity limited by scribe, 20 people, 60 ideas in 30 minutes.
- Extroverts empowered as their ideas are captured - introverts struggle.
- Up to 20 participants.
- Typical duration from 4 hours to 1-2 days.
- Break-out groups used to make sessions personal.
- Planning to ensure the session runs smoothly and achieves the goals.
- All participants working on a digital whiteboard (optional).

Underpinning the new era of collaboration is the use of digital whiteboards.

In recent years, this technology has progressed significantly and developed into sophisticated and flexible collaboration boards that capture people's thoughts.

People in the same room

"Collaboration and confidence empower people's creativity to shine through."

Actor

Collaboration mantras

Guiding principles

To harness the value of collaboration, ensure these guiding principles set the standard for your behaviors and attitudes when collaborating.

Successful collaborators continually recite these mantras, so they become part of day to day thinking and interwoven within all work.

- Work in parallel to maximize collaboration.
- Over prepare and over prepare.
- Treat collaboration like a series of sprints.
- Be visual in everything you do.
- Change your game to be on top of your game.

Mantra

Download your own set of Method Cards. Link can be found in the resource section.

"Revising a key corporate document that touches every aspect of a business can be a daunting prospect. Overlay engaging a large stakeholder group from across the globe within a compressed timeframe and you have a challenge! My team understands the importance of collaboration and the passion comes through in every aspect of what they do.

The approach we took was not only unique, but highly productive and engaging. In my case, by working collectively (and mostly in silence) in a virtual environment close to 850 ideas were generated by approx. 80 people to enhance the document. It was incredible to witness people so focused on the task and having fun. In all honesty, I was skeptical at the start of the process. It was hard to see how it would work! In the end the results spoke for themselves."

Principal Advisor

Collaboration
campaign in action

Work in parallel

"Collaborate asynchronously to climb on each other's shoulders."

Always:

- Exploit the virtual space to enable collaborators to contribute to the shared space independently and in their own time – asynchronously.
- Set clear protocols around expectations, scope of work and communication.
- Be disciplined in allocation of short sharp time durations to ensure focus and efficiency.
- Use visual forms of communication that can be shared and actioned asynchronously.
- Build a culture of continuous improvement through the power of incubation and shared ownership.
- Include regular synchronous check-ins.

Work in parallel

Over prepare and over prepare

"Over prepare, over prepare and over prepare."

Always:

- Accept remote sessions require more planning than traditional face to face sessions.
- Believe more pre-work leads to better sessions.
- Design engagement into sessions to ensure everyone can participate equally.
- Acknowledge remote conditions are more difficult to manage.
- Become comfortable with how the tools work.
- Build in contingency time to get people onto the virtual board.
- Be ready to troubleshoot as things will go wrong.

"As individuals we make sound, when we collaborate, we make music".

Professional Musician

Over prepare and over prepare

It's a sprint

"Treat it like a series of sprints."

Always:

- Include time for people to get to know each other prior to a session.
- Break up a campaign into a series of 30 minutes, 1- or 2-hour sprints.
- Measure in minute intervals and watch the clock.
- Time box everything - pre-work, presentations, activities, breaks and feedback – everything.
- Pack the agenda to ensure a sense of urgency, so everyone is fully engaged.
- Use group work of 3-4 people so they can hold each other accountable and on task.
- Have warm-up exercises at the start to get people ready to sprint through the activities.

It's a sprint

Be visual

"Be visual in everything you do."

Always:

- Learn to be visual! It's worked for 30,000 years.
- Make activities visual and personal to promote memory, create clarity and fire the imagination.
- Create a visual language to link with the visual wiring within our brain.
- Use images to improve recall, creativity and understanding regardless of spoken language.
- Build a visual glossary of icons to provide immediate non-verbal feedback in silence.
- Use visuals to help guide and focus discussions if people don't understand or disagree.

Be visual

"Collaboration is seeing the big picture."

Hospitality Manager

Change your game

"Change your game to be on top of your game."

Always:

- Stay ahead of expectations by mixing things up and changing your game.
- Adopt a digital mindset to engage and harness the virtual world.
- Continually learn, grow and reflect to stop the inevitable decline.
- Take time to let your thoughts incubate, allowing your subconscious mind to do the work.
- Experiment with collaboration, don't be scared, find new ways to make it better.
- Continue to look for new technologies to refine and enhance people's experience.

Change your game

"We collaborate because big things can't be done on a small scale."

Olympian

Collaboration essentials

These collaboration essentials underpin effective collaboration. They are necessary and the first step to collaborating in a virtual world. Be sure to embrace these essentials and make them integral to your collaboration efforts.

Fostering a digital mind

Applying the art of facilitation

Using virtual whiteboard

"We designed and facilitated a program which brought together a wide range of subject matter experts from across the company to create a vision for a future state.

We were initially concerned about the challenges of running a complex process involving a large group across multiple time zones, but the process design and tools were well suited to the job.

The work was broken down into a number of sessions to keep energy levels high. The format and facilitation was engaging and relevant. Feedback was positive from all involved, including a great pool of ideas and thinking to define the future."

Environmental Manager

Collaboration
campaign in action

"Collaboration produces ideas and ideas change the world."

Police Officer

Digital mind essential

To drive effective virtual collaboration by improving remote work using a digital mindset.

Successful collaborators:

- Fully exploit the digital world by bringing together virtual teams, tools and techniques.
- Harness the full potential of the virtual world and its technology.
- Bring people together from different backgrounds and cultures to share knowledge and experience and to combine their efforts to solve problems.

"We know we must change, but how we do it is the challenge."

Meteorologist

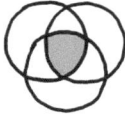

Digital sweet spot

Connectivity

Psychology of collaboration

Fostering a digital mind

Digital sweet spot

To fully exploit the digital world by bringing together virtual teams, tools and techniques.

Explore and embrace a digital mindset.

Prepare for and engage in the remote working environment.

Embrace virtual tools and remote interaction.

Pursue and use virtual techniques to create positive remote experiences.

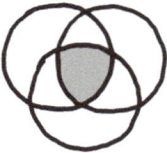

Harness the power of incubation when working remotely.

Digital sweet spot

Connectivity

To harness the full potential of the virtual world and its technology.

Maximise time zones.

Have reliable and effective audio.

Connect with people using video.

Have the right computer set-up "Be visual in everything you do".

Help people feel comfortable when working from home.

Connectivity

Psychology of collaboration

To bring people from different backgrounds
and cultures together to share knowledge
and experience and to combine their
efforts to solve problems.

Practise honesty, trust and
respect.

Recognise, accept and
manage conflict within
normal collaboration.

Recognise and work
with people's emotional
triggers.

Identify and manage
the stages of team
development.

Psychology of
collaboration

Recognise and celebrate
cultural awareness.

Art of facilitation essential

To enable effective collaboration through productive and meaningful remote conversations that build alignment, clarity and focus.

Successful collaborators:

- Collaborate using productive and meaningful conversations so everyone's thoughts are captured and discussed.
- Focus on the right topics and maximise people's contribution.

Facilitation craft

Workshop design

Trouble shooting

Art of facilitation

Facilitation craft

To ensure collaboration is productive and meaningful so that everyone's thoughts are captured and discussed.

Create a meaningful space.

Open and close activities.

Capture inputs and outputs.

Optimise alignment.

Become remote ready.

Model positive and constructive behaviours.

Facilitation craft

Workshop design

To ensure collaboration is focused on the right topics and maximises people's contribution.

Assign roles.

Utilise remote friendly methods.

Prepare for the virtual session.

Effectively deliver virtual sessions.

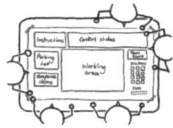

Create user friendly workstations.

Utilise break out groups.

Workshop design

Troubleshooting

To optimise virtual collaboration by actively engaging and managing people and technology during sessions.

Troubleshoot to ensure:

 Energised, excited and enthusiastic people who are not bored.

 Alert, attentive, observant and mindful people who are not distracted.

 Timing is optimised and effectively managed to create a sense of urgency.

 Technology failure is minimised and managed.

 Good, reliable and consistent internet connection.

 Quiet, peaceful and silent workspace.

Trouble shooting

Whiteboard essential

To provide a large and flexible workspace that fosters creativity while showing people's thinking in real-time.

Successful collaborators:

- Improve productivity, connection and trust using digital whiteboards.
- Collaborate on the board in real-time to provide instant feedback.
- Work on the whiteboard in parallel to accelerate progress.
- Use remote methods and templates to facilitate collaboration.
- Maintain the whiteboard and publish the outcomes.

Whiteboard

Visual collaboration

Using visuals when collaborating brings the bigger picture into view and builds shared language, ownership and commitment for a group dealing with complex challenges.

Believe in the value of visual collaboration.

Use images to connect with others.

Use a common visual language.

Visual collaboration

Whiteboard types

Digital whiteboards provide the infinite space where people collaborate in real time to enhance engagement and solve problems. They can be tailored with structure and headings to fulfil different purposes. The following are some common board types:

Develop project boards to define, manage and deliver projects.

Deliver compelling and interactive presentations using whiteboards.

Facilitate productive and meaningful conversations using workshop boards.

Document and share outcomes in real-time on a dashboard.

Project boards make up most of the digital collaboration space. This is where all the work happens. Using the iceberg analogy, over 90% of the work happens below the water level. This is where people come onto the digital whiteboard to advance ideas and work.

Workboards

PRESENTATION BOARD

WORKSHOP BOARD

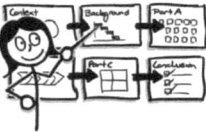

DASHBOARD

PROJECT BOARD

The evolution of collaborating with digital whiteboards:

- Starts with the project board, where you and your colleagues let content grow organically but reorganize it now and again.
- Next, you may want to pop your head above the water and share content from your project board by creating and sharing a presentation board.
- Typically, you now update your project board based on the presentation feedback.
- In some cases, you may need to involve external stakeholders and run a specific session creating and using a workshop board.
- Once again, you will update your project board based on the workshop feedback.
- You may even create a dashboard to plan and monitor your collaboration efforts.

"We collaborate to make a job easier and faster."

Year 6 Student

Digital whiteboard

A digital whiteboard takes the concept of the physical whiteboard to the next level. You are no longer limited to being in the same room; people can collaborate in real-time from anywhere in the world. While any sketch app could function as a digital whiteboard, several platforms offer features to improve the quality and efficiency of work.

The best digital whiteboards include:

- Unlimited canvas
- Commenting tools
- Sticky note features
- Multiple export options
- File and image uploading
- Easy access

Why use a digital whiteboard

Digital whiteboards allow teams to collaborate remotely. An advantage of this is the ability to work both synchronously and asynchronously. The best digital whiteboards can have teams working on the same whiteboard at the same time.

This is synchronous collaboration. You can work together in real-time; as one person types, another can make a note, bring in an image, or draw up a graph. You can give and receive instant feedback.

Asynchronous collaboration is the work done by others when you are offline. The digital whiteboards allow everyone to add their ideas in their own time; this means that work can be done around the clock by taking advantage of different time zones. By engaging and involving people around the world you are not limited to the usual 9-5 work hours.

Digital whiteboard

Good digital whiteboards consider:

- Accessibility so someone can easily access the board the first time and thereafter.
- Usability so someone can easily learn to use the board and improve work efficiency, for example, button layout, shortcuts and readability.
- Design tools to allow you to design a board, for example, drawing, marker colour, mind mapping, templates, drag and drop, canvas size and sticky note features.
- Export options that are useful and easy to use, for example, excel, pdf and images.
- Collaboration tools to enhance collaboration by enabling you to work with someone to produce work, for example, communication features, commenting tools, track changes and multiple people working.
- Facilitation tools to provide facilitators with the ability to lead the group, for example, 'follow me' function.

"Collaboration brings efficiencies as you can copy others' ideas."

Resource Manager

Working remotely on digital whiteboard

"Collaboration and teamwork go hand in hand and the output from a team is more than an individual."

Mathematician

Campaign interactions

It's important to consider who should be involved in the campaign as this will influence the type of campaign and interactions, for example, virtual, hybrid or face to face. It's very common to have multiple stakeholders located across multiple locations with varying numbers of participants during a collaboration campaign.

The following dimensions provide a framework to assess who should be involved and how they could interact.

Stakeholder diversity

Location

Participants

Campaign interactions

"The global pandemic has significantly influenced the way we now interact as a business. The inability to meet 'face to face' has necessitated the need to be innovative. As such, remote working has become the norm rather than the exception. The collaborative campaign was a challenging initiative in that many parts of the business needed to come together.

Remote delivery via the Miro board delivered a practical solution, allowing our many parts to come together virtually to contribute a rich range of inputs in a highly effective and efficient manner. In a time-poor environment, this style of campaigning was just what was needed to enable insights that would have arguably been prohibitive using the typical meet and greet approach."

Senior Manager

Collaboration
campaign in action

"Even if you are challenged, it's still a chance to reflect. Suppose you win over a disagreeing person; what an ally."

Executive Assistant

Stakeholder diversity

Stakeholders provide the drive and momentum required for successful collaboration. A stakeholder is a person or group who:

- Is responsible for the final decision.
- Is positively or negatively affected by the collaboration.
- Has expertise or resources to significantly impact the quality, cost, schedule and acceptance of the collaboration work.
- Has organisational influence.

The selection of stakeholders is frequently driven by the scope of the collaboration – what needs to be discussed, is it tactical, strategic or policy driven?

The greater the diversity the more complex the collaboration campaign.

For example, when collaborating the levels of diversity can be described in the following ways.

Stakeholder diversity

One team
Typically made up of individuals who work on a day-to-day basis; they are tactical, focused on business-as-usual and have an existing relationship.

One department
Typically made up of different teams whose individuals may work together across teams to align around common goals, although individuals are unlikely to have strong relationships across teams.

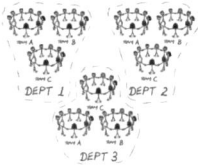

Multiple departments
Typically a combination of departments with different goals. Naturally, each department is made up of teams. The departments typically interact at the leadership level, where relationships may have been developed. It is very unlikely that individuals across department teams have relationships.

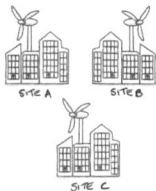

Multiple sites
Typically a combination of different sites with different business goals. Typically, each site has multiple departments and teams. The sites may interact at the CEO level. It's rare for individual team members to have relationships across multiple sites.

One department

Location

The location of workers has a significant
impact on the collaboration type, being
remote, hybrid or face to face collaboration.
A bigger spread of locations also leads
to diverse groups in terms of culture and
perspectives. The greater the spread the
more complex the collaboration campaign.
People working in the same office are
typically very aligned around customs and
norms, while people spread across the
world will speak different languages, work
in different time zones and have different
cultural norms.

For example, the spread of working
locations can be considered in the following
ways.

Same office
Where people come together to
collaborate. It's very easy to arrange as
people just walk down the hall or catch
an elevator to the next floor and start
collaborating.

Same city
Where people from within that office
collaborate with people making the trip
across the city to work together. It is easy
to arrange, the locals walk down the hall,
while the visitors travel a short distance to
be in a common space.

Location

Same state and country

Where people are now more broadly dispersed. It is difficult for people travelling within the state and moreso for interstate people as they will incur travel time, flights and accommodation costs to collaborate. Often people away from the home location and city become remote participants.

Internationally spread

Where travel between countries is very difficult to arrange and collaboration will incur significant lead time, travel time and flights and accommodation costs. Often people away from the home location and city become remote participants.

Internationally spread

Participants

The number of participants has a significant impact on logistics in terms of lead team and costs to arrange the collaboration and the ability to be flexible with dates. The more people involved, the more complex the collaboration campaign. For example, when collaborating the number of participants can be considered in the following ways.

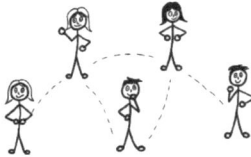

Zero to five people
Typically easy to arrange as people can make themselves available.

10 people
A little more difficult, conflicting dates make accessing people harder.

Participants

20 people
Normally requires a few months lead time to secure participants availability.

30 people and above
Requires three months lead time and focused effort to organise and coordinate participants. It is a major body of work.

People connecting

Campaign interaction selection

The following summary combines stakeholder diversity, location and participants to help guide whether the collaboration interaction is virtual, hybrid or face to face.

Virtual Interaction

- Multiple sites or external to the business
- Same country or international
- 30 and above people

Considerations:

- Policy collaboration is typically done virtually as sites are geographically spread around the country or world.
- Collaborating with external companies is generally for a particular reason to help learn from each other and build new insights. This is typically done virtually.
- If people are located around the state, country and the world, this requires significant costs to bring people together - hence virtual interaction is an option.
- As the numbers increase, so do the logistics around dates, travel time and costs. Flying twenty people to a face-to-face session can become expensive. A virtual interaction becomes very cost-effective and practical.
- Once the numbers get beyond twenty, a virtual interaction begins to shine as very productive sessions can be facilitated with up to 100 people.

Virtual interaction

Hybrid Interaction

- One or multiple departments or sites
- Same city, state or country
- 10 to 20 people

Considerations:

- Hybrid interaction is possible; combining face-to-face interaction people in the home location and city, virtual interaction with people from interstate or overseas.
- When designing a hybrid interaction, always design for the remote participants as face-to-face often looks after itself.

Hybrid interactions

Face to face Interaction

- One team or department.
- Same office or city
- 5 to 10 people

Considerations:

- Tactical collaboration is typically done face-to-face at a team and department level since they are generally in the same location.
- Strategic collaboration is typically done face-to-face across multiple departments since they are generally in the same location.
- If stakeholders are in the same city, then a face-to-face interaction is an option.
- Having 5 people means its logistically practical to have face-to-face interaction, even if they must travel.

Face to face
interaction

Campaign roles

Once the scope and participants have been agreed upon, it's possible to identify their role within the campaign. A simple RACI (Responsible, Accountable, Consulted and Informed) describes each participant's level of engagement within the collaboration. For example:

Responsible
A person(s) delivering the campaign, whose role is to:
- Set up
- Establish scope
- Create design
- Facilitate campaign

Accountable
A person accountable for the campaign, whose role is to:
- Provide direction
- Remove barriers
- Kick off campaign
- Remain involved

Consulted
A person(s) actively participating in the campaign, whose role is to:
- Provide ideas
- Review work
- Provide feedback

Informed
A person(s) who is kept informed on the campaign progress, whose role is to:
- Review campaign communications
- Talk about the campaign

Knowing participants' roles helps with mapping people to collaboration activities.

Campaign roles

"We collaborate to look at problems through different perspectives."

Student

Campaign timeline

Campaign timeline

A campaign is typically spaced over several weeks and includes focused, short and sharp sessions, facilitated on a digital whiteboard. By spacing the sessions people can incubate and reflect, creating new insights into the problem.

The number of sessions depends on the scope of the collaboration; the more scope, the more collaboration time. The type of session interaction (virtual, hybrid or face-to- face) depends on stakeholder diversity, location and number of participants.

A typical collaboration timeline is shown below. The timeline maps common campaign sessions, including a collaboration kickoff, working and alignment sessions. At the end of each session, a review is completed to reflect on the output and help to design the next session's scope. A session recap is also communicated back to all participants to maintain energy and momentum.

A typical two week collaborating process:

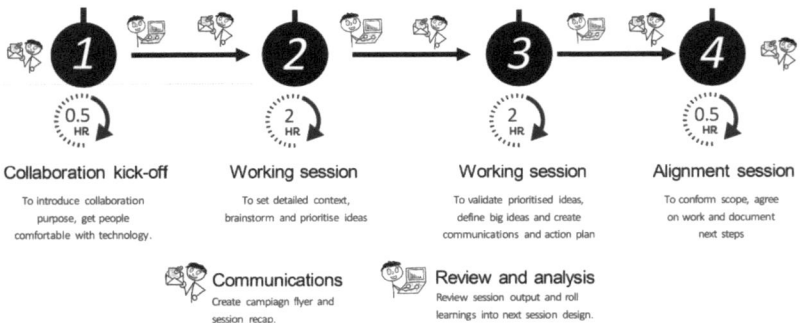

1	2	3	4
0.5 HR	2 HR	2 HR	0.5 HR
Collaboration kick-off	**Working session**	**Working session**	**Alignment session**
To introduce collaboration purpose, get people comfortable with technology.	To set detailed context, brainstorm and prioritise ideas	To validate prioritised ideas, define big ideas and create communications and action plan	To conform scope, agree on work and document next steps

Communications
Create campaign flyer and session recap.

Review and analysis
Review session output and roll learnings into next session design.

"With the move to Webex for all meetings last year, I could see engagement decline within large groups. People stopped contributing in groups greater than five, there would be one dominant voice – then silence.

So, when organising a collaboration of 20 technical experts across the country to do work beyond their job, be creative and build a new concept using a virtual platform, I wasn't confident that it would be successful.

By designing a bespoke virtual program, we achieved success beyond my expectations – and better than I think we could have achieved in person. We have a quality, collaboratively-built product, that has sign-off from technical experts... and senior management."

Environmental Lead

Collaboration
campaign in action

Collaboration campaign planning

An effective collaboration campaign requires significant effort and planning. The campaign design is an interactive process, as each interaction helps to shape and drive the design of the next interaction. The following meetings are typically 60 minutes each and underpin a successful campaign.

A campaign always commences with a kickoff meeting to map out the high-level scope and timing. This meeting gives a sense of confidence as everyone is on the same page. The concept design meeting empowers creative and divergent thinking as people explore possible approaches to the campaign. The preliminary design meeting confirms a possible approach and outlines the overall campaign activities, timing and expected outcomes.

Detail design meetings occurs prior to each collaboration session. Each meeting confirms the detailed steps and minute by minute activities. The uniqueness of a campaign approach is that the outputs from one individual session feed the next collaboration session. This design process ensures conversations are productive and meaningful and always focus on what's most important.

**Campaign
meetings**

| Kick off to plan and agree on the overall scope, timing and expectations | → | Concept design to identify various creative approaches to address the purpose | → | Preliminary design to focus on the preferred approach and techniques | → | Detail design to confirm final design and align team |

The road test meetings also occur prior to each collaboration session. The meeting walks through the detailed agenda to ensure everyone knows their role and what can go wrong.

The collaboration session is where the work gets done. All the previous planning and meetings ensure people are fully engaged, motivated and energized. The session is a safe space where everyone's voices can be heard in delivering an integrated body of work.

Constant communications are fundamental to a successful campaign. It maintains interest and commitment to the collaboration purpose. At the conclusion of each session a short recap is sent to all participants, summarising the outcome and thanking them for their contribution. The close out meeting occurs at the end of the campaign to close out any outstanding items, capture next steps and any lessons learnt.

A campaign can be virtual, hybrid or face-to-face. Alternatively, it is very common to mix up the collaboration types as part of a campaign. For example, a virtual kick off session, followed by face-to-face and remote working sessions and a remote close out session.

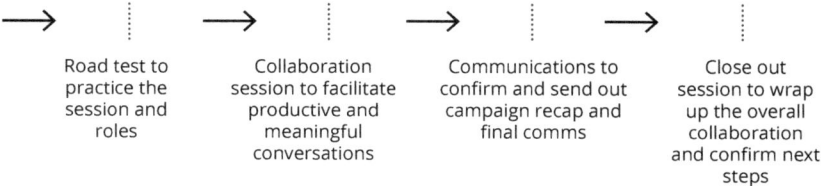

| Road test to practice the session and roles | Collaboration session to facilitate productive and meaningful conversations | Communications to confirm and send out campaign recap and final comms | Close out session to wrap up the overall collaboration and confirm next steps |

Collaboration threats and rewards

Be mindful

In a fifth of a second, our subconscious brain automatically recognises social triggers to approach (primary rewards) or avoid (primary threats).

The approach-avoid (sometimes called fight or flight) response dramatically affects our perceptions, problem-solving, decision-making, stress management, collaboration and motivation.

As we engage in a digital world, it's important to recognise and reflect on how you and your colleagues will be impacted. Some people will see many rewards while others see only threats.

Through our research, we identified the typical rewards and threats driving virtual, hybrid and face-to-face collaboration. When designing a collaboration campaign, your goal is to maximise the rewards and manage the threats people experience.

The following summary provides useful insights into collaborating in a digital world.

"In the current time there is a trend, and in some cases a necessity, to work remotely and in isolation from the rest of our team. This is particularly true since the COVID-19 pandemic impacted the way we interact with others. Meanwhile there are several benefits in this new way to live or study or work. Certainly there are a few challenges to maintain the cohesion and motivation of any team. This highlights the importance of working collaboratively and using several techniques to improve the way that we collaborate with our team members taking advantages of digital solutions."

Resource Manager

Collaboration
campaign in action

Virtual collaboration rewards and threats

Virtual collaboration rewards allow participants to:

- Engage with the best, most diverse people with divergent ideas while expanding our own horizons within a virtual world.
- Maintain a work/life balance with increased autonomy and flexibility to get work done.
- Enable new learning by re-imagining work, solving problems and up-skilling through personal growth.
- Make a difference through faster turnaround, effective work sessions and asynchronously working in real-time across time zones.
- Re-imagine the future by building a sustainable business through re-imagining collaboration within a virtual world.

Virtual collaboration threats may cause participants to:

- Confront unknowns, having thoughts of being left out, feeling lost with virtual technology.
- Deal with change, lack of confidence and feeling overwhelmed working in the virtual world.
- Struggle with digital/work fatigue, distractions and a lack of focus and inspiration.
- Experience poor relationships, not being able to pick up non-verbal cues, nor read the room or body language.
- Battle technology failures, poor bandwidth, poor connectivity and frustration while needing more technical support.

"Virtual rewards revolve around accessing people and a positive work/life balance."

"Virtual threats revolve around dealing with technological change."

Hybrid collaboration rewards and threats

Hybrid collaboration rewards

As face-to-face participants we:
- Build and foster teamwork both within the session and over dinner.
- Work in our time zone as we all meet in a common location.
- See the bigger picture by observing the diversity of remote participants.

As virtual participants we:
- Are still involved and can contribute.
- Are the right people with the right skills, as it's easy to dial in another person.
- Appreciate office dynamics by observing how face-to-face participants work.

"Hybrid rewards revolve around involving the right people, either face to face or virtually"

Hybrid collaboration threats

As face-to-face participants we:
- Take control of the collaboration and inadvertently ignore remote participants.
- Have side conversations alienating remote participants.
- Are frustrated with technology by not being able to see and hear remote participants.

As virtual participants we:
- Feel second class as compared with face-to-face participants due to power imbalance.
- Disconnect as it's challenging to hear or see face-to-face participants.
- Are frustrated with technology when it fails as we feel silly and not valued.

"Hybrid threats revolve around virtual participants feeling like second class citizens"

"Face-to-face rewards revolve around team building, emotions and connections"

Face-to-face collaboration rewards and threats

Face-to-face rewards

As participants we:
- Build a sense of community, cohesion and belonging through side meetings.
- Develop a shared understanding of goals and a larger purpose for how people can contribute.
- Foster a deeper understanding of the hosting environment and office culture.
- Provide instant feedback as people can ask questions and get answers.
- Build personal connections where ideas, cooperation and respect flow.

Face-to-face threats

As participants we:
- Take up lots of time when you factor in the loss of productivity through travel time.
- Are not cost-effective as people are required to book flights, accommodation and maybe a venue to host the meeting.
- Are not the right people with the right skills as logistics limit how many and who should attend.
- Are difficult to access since meetings are typically 1-2 days minimum to justify the travel costs of bringing people together.
- Lose momentum as the meeting can take months to arrange and is often delayed to secure participants.
- Lose efficiency as people are often sidetracked in face to face conversations.

"Face-to-face threats revolve around accessing the right people, travel time and costs"

"I collaborate, because other people can bring things to the piece of music."

Hip Hop Musician

Collaboration obstacles

Our collaboration training program revealed obstacles around moving collaboration into the virtual space. We identified psychological and logistical obstacles preventing people from making the transition to a virtual world. They ideas fell into three main categories: environment, preparation and skills.

Underpinning a successful transition to the virtual world is an aspiration to:

- Foster an environment where people have the right skills to confidently work virtually.
- Become competent in virtual collaboration to show what is possible.
- Acknowledge peoples mental and physical circumstances when collaborating virtually.
- Commit time and effort to learning new skills.

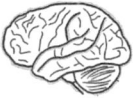

Psychological

Logistical

Psychological
Logistical

Source: Tri Helix Collaboration Training program. 110 obstacles identified from 60 interviews across the world.

Make use of the following strategies to overcome collaboration obstacles.

Environment

*   Design a workspace for yourself with limited distractions that enables you to perform to the best of your abilities.
*   Create a welcoming and comfortable virtual environment that reduces people's fears and anxieties about going virtual.
*   Commit yourself to working virtually by being present for all sessions, coming in with the same mindset you would for in person work.

Workspace

Preparation

*   Select a virtual platform that is accessible by all and can be used for the foreseeable future.
*   Have a clear design that is communicated and balances information and interaction such that everyone's voice can be heard.
*   Schedule so everyone can attend the sessions, having consideration for time zones and personal commitments.

Virtual platforms

Skills

*   Confidently present and lead a virtual session, react to situations and get the best out of your participants.
*   Use the virtual programs and navigate the board/session in a confident and competent manner.
*   React to technical difficulties during the session, implementing processes to ensure the session runs smoothly.

Lead from the front

**Virtual Mantras
Method Cards**

**Digital Mind
Method Cards**

**Art of Facilitation
Method Cards**

**Visual Whiteboard
Method Cards**

**Campaign Planning
Method Cards**

All resources are located at www.trihelix.com.au/resources

Download resource packs (PDF)

Working Virtually Poster

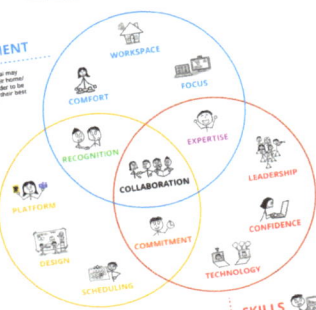

**Virtual
Work Obstacles
Poster**

All resources are located at www.trihelix.com.au/resources

Download resource packs (PDF)

Collaboration Poster

All resources are located at www.trihelix.com.au/resources

"A song writer needs a producer, a fashion designer needs someone to make the clothes and a writer needs someone to print the book. We always need others to progress our work."

Disability Advocate

Part 3 -
What is
collaboration

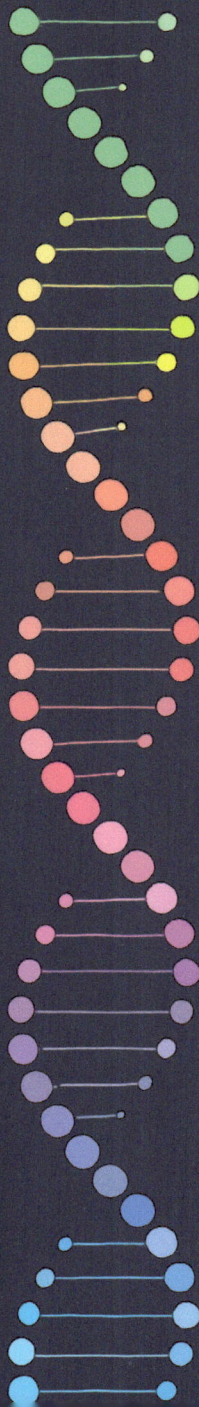

Collaboration scope

Now we know what collaboration in a digital world looks like with its associated threats and rewards, it's important to consider the scope of a collaboration campaign.

The scope describes what the collaboration is trying to achieve. It helps to set boundaries by confirming what's in and out of the collaboration. For example, will the collaboration produce:

- Ideas and improvement?
- Alignment and shared understanding?
- Connections based on affinity and trust?
- Engagement to motivate and inspire?
- Results that make sense and are helpful?
- A combination of all these outcomes?

The key to any successful collaboration is to explore the scope upfront. It's best to involve some of the collaboration team so they can contribute and start to take ownership. This builds confidence, motivation and a common purpose.

The scope has a significant impact on a collaboration campaign. It directly influences the type of collaboration - virtual, hybrid or face-to-face - and the overall duration of the campaign. Naturally, the bigger the scope, the more collaboration is required.

The scope also influences how people interact. Choices include formal, informal or a combination. They may be narrow within your team or broad across industries and the world. The scope drives many decisions when designing a collaboration campaign.

With the scope formed and the types of interactions decided, collaboration rests on the variety and rigour of conversations.

Conversations

Collaboration success

Collaboration success has always been built on conversations. It's how we communicate and share ideas verbally, visually, or digitally.

Conversations are part of our human design and essential to our survival; it's listening, agreeing and disagreeing. It's how we operate as a collective to deliver better outcomes. Conversations allow us to connect, build relationships and feel good.

At times conversations can be challenging. We have learn that successful collaborations using a third point of reference make conversations more meaningful and productive. For example, using a white board, piece of paper or sharing computer screens can remove the awkwardness. It shifts the focus to a third point to help people to remain focused.

We have also observed that successful collaborations engage in various types of conversations. For example, a successful team **facilitates** **open** conversations where people can think differently, discuss the **technical** work behind the collaboration outcomes and explore how the outcomes are **accepted** and owned by the team.

Third point
of reference

These types of conversations are deliberately broad and consider topics with a focus on:

- Being organised.
- Fostering a growth mindset.
- Creating inspiration.
- Harnessing people's knowledge.
- Establishing and managing projects.
- Improving how we work.
- Building ownership.
- Developing affinity.

Over the years, we have built an extensive suite of conversation topics that can act as this third point of reference (150+ and growing). These topics are facilitated to build openness, deliver the technical work and ensure acceptance of the technical work in hearts and minds.

These topics within a collaboration campaign form the scope. The more topics to be explored, the longer the campaign. It's important to note, every collaboration campaign will require facilitation and involve open, technical work and acceptance conversations, the mix will depend on the overall focus of the campaign.

Tri Helix have developed a simple success formula and delivery model to ensure the right conversations happen at the right time within any collaboration.

Types

Topics

Success formula

$$\text{Success} = F\,(T+A)$$

The success formula describes the relationship between the various types of conversations required for a successful collaboration.

Facilitation is fundamental as it influences and amplifies **openness**, **technical** work and **acceptance** work. Facilitation work describes the planning and delivery of meaningful conversations. The better the facilitation work, the better the conversations amongst the team, leading to improved solutions, technical work outcomes and levels of acceptance.

The formula shows that effective facilitation fosters openness around the technical work and acceptance work. This openness allows people to think differently, to look for better solutions by applying a growth mindset, to be inspired and generate new ideas.

The facilitation work also builds acceptance of the technical work in people's hearts and minds.

For example, as a team, have you ever:

- Written a document that no-one read?
- Created a detailed plan that was not followed?
- Introduced a process that was rejected?

Facilitation

How successful was your team? These simple examples share the importance of acceptance. The truth is, without acceptance, success is impossible. Hence, its existence must never be taken for granted.

In these examples, as a team, it is easy to get caught up in the quality of the technical work and not facilitate acceptance. A mistake is to think there is acceptance. It's best to always investigate a little further and engage with the team to understand how they feel and what they really want and to take a more collaborative approach.

Therefore, you need to routinely check what members are thinking. Are they attending review meetings and are you monitoring how much red pen is appearing on their work? This will immediately highlight the actual level of team openness and acceptance and provide a 'wake up' call to raise the level of engagement so that openness and acceptance is assured.

From now on within your team, consciously bind the openness, technical work and acceptance together and amplify it with a facilitative approach outlined in the success formula.

It might feel strange at first and a little uncomfortable. Typically, when you start, you are worried that the facilitation will take up more of your management time. However, with persistence, the teamwork will be more successful.

"Interacting with a focus on a common purpose produces alignment and clarity."

Health care worker

Low acceptance

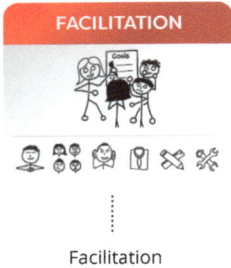

Facilitation

Delivery model

Collaboration success requires we **facilitate** **open**, productive and meaningful conversations, exploring both the **technical work** and people's **acceptance** of the outcomes.

The scope of these important conversations are described below.

Facilitation

Bring the best out of people:

- Amplify the openness and acceptance of technical work in people's hearts and minds.
- Be self-aware and genuinely care about your team.
- Prepare for and deliver meaningful and productive conversations.
- Ensure conversations are safe, open and non-judgmental.

Openness

Go beyond the obvious:

- Challenge, sharpen and redirect thinking towards provocative and radical ideas.
- Make problem- solving creative, fun and repeatable.
- Establish a desire to change by being motivated and learning from others.
- Harness the collective knowledge of a group and funnel their thinking to deliver an agreed, prioritised set of actions.

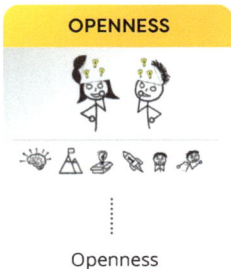

Openness

Technical Work

Deliver tangible outputs:

- Plan, organise, secure and manage resources.
- Ensure successful completion of goals.
- Deliver the scope as promised.
- Take an idea from start to finish to realise the benefits to the business.

Acceptance

Establish urgency and commitment:

- Ensure all the technical work is undertaken meaningfully.
- Establish acceptance in people's hearts and minds at a subconscious level.
- Bring people together from different backgrounds and cultures.
- Share knowledge and experience and combine their efforts to solve problems.

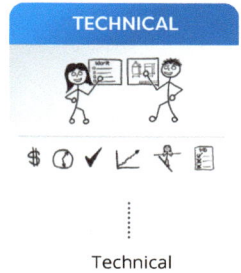

TECHNICAL

Technical

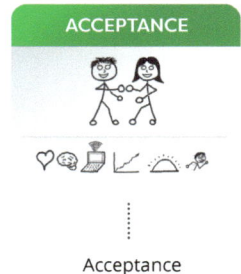

ACCEPTANCE

Acceptance

"The story is
not complete
until we have
everyone's
input."

Flight Attendant

Shift your focus

A manager must consistently **facilitate** the project and regulate the degree of emphasis directed to the **openness**, **technical work** and **acceptance** work according to the project stage.

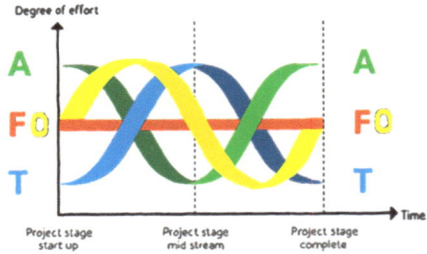

The diagram above shows the ebb and flow of focus for each of the four components of the success formula. It shows a high focus on, acceptance work at the beginning of a project as this is when the team need to be engaged. Then the, openness work ramps up as it inspires the team with new insights and motivation, leading to a strong focus on ideation which drives the technical work with has increased focus throughout the middle stages. Then, towards the end, the focus must shift back to acceptance to ensure strong ownership and acceptance of the outcomes.

Shift your
focus

The effort directed to facilitation work remains constant throughout the project because it binds openness, technical work and acceptance work together.

Shifting focus to apply the right mix helps ensure collaboration and project success.

Constant facilitation effort

Team success scenarios

Facilitation scenarios help to apply the appropriate mix at the right time and can be used along the project journey. These scenarios are already documented as part of many organisations' processes. Each scenario sets out objectives, activities and tools. Some are used only once while others are repeated at different stages of the project journey.

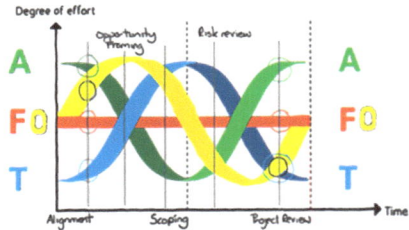

The diagram above shows how five scenarios have been used in a project. An alignment session occurs early in a project to build common understanding around the project objectives and how the team will work together. This is at a time when acceptance needs are high. As the technical focus ramps up it is best to run an opportunity framing session which is designed to identify a number of viable options that will be investigated within the project.

A technical scoping session is run to confirm the project scope, assign resources and identify critical interfaces. At the peak of the technical focus a risk review is completed to identify the major risks to the project.

As the project is nearing its end the collaboration's focus shifts back to acceptance, so a project review with the sponsor enables you to seek endorsement.

Alignment scenario

As discussed earlier, the focus of collaboration shifts throughout the various stages of a project. This is depicted below by the coloured bars. Facilitation (red) remains constant throughout the project, however, openness (yellow), technical work (blue) and acceptance (green) shift in focus as the project progresses.

Project alignment

Our project team is in place and we are kicking off (or underway) and we are not aligned. There are unrealistic goals, people are resisting tasks and there is increased tension. We need to quickly align and build the team.

Opportunity framing

We are kicking off a study and people already have a preconceived solution. We are heading down a path that will lead to rework and we are forced to circle back and look at better alternatives. We need to frame the opportunity and find a few viable alternatives to study.

Project scoping

Our project team is forming. It is unclear who is delivering what, who needs information from whom and what work is critical. We need to confirm and agree on the scope.

Risk review

The project is underway. We can't afford any surprises and must start to prioritise and manage our risks. We need a solid risk register to drive our work.

Risk review scenario

Success framework

The Success Framework is depicted below.

At its core is the Success Formula, representing the four conversation types - facilitation, openness, technical work and acceptance - and their relationship. Flowing out of the Success Formula are eight elements describing possible conversations.

The conversations begin with facilitation work and being organised, followed by openness work designed to foster a growth mindset, inspiration and ideation. Next, there is the technical conversations around projects and improvement and, finally, the acceptance work focused on building ownership and affinity.

The Success Framework and its eight elements provide a third point of reference to begin the important collaboration conversations.

Success framework

Success mindmap

The Success Mindmap describes the hierarchy of elements, sub elements and tools within the four conversation types.

There are 28 sub-elements spread across the eight elements. Within each sub-element there are additional (not shown in the mind map).

There are more than 150 conversation tools, each describing its purpose, benefits and use to ensure team conversations are productive and meaningful.

The Success Mindmap, and each of its hierarchy headings provide a third point of reference to begin the important team conversations.

The remainder of this document expands and describes each element's intent, purpose, sub- elements and conversation tools.

Scan to view and download our team framework and mindmap guides

Success mind map

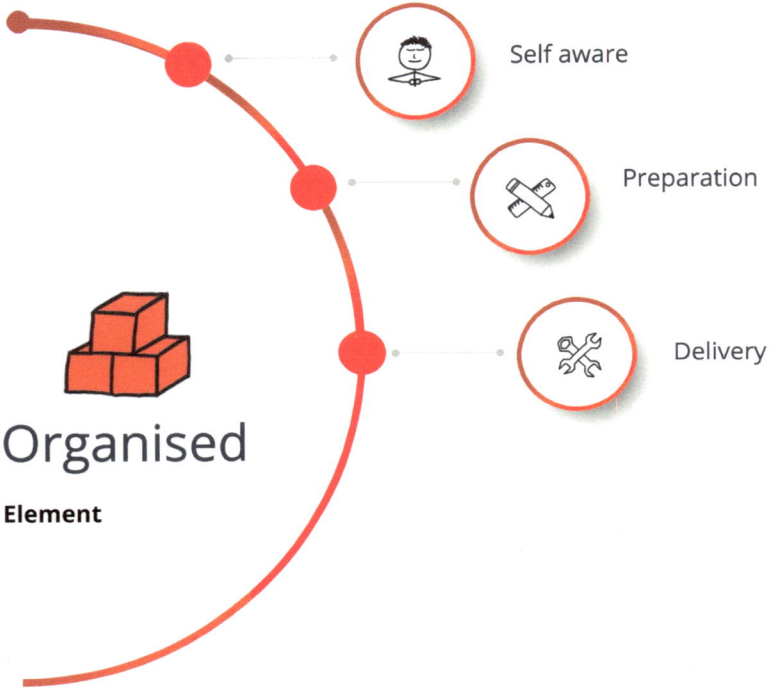

Self aware

Preparation

Delivery

Organised

Element

Organised

Being organised amplifies the openness and acceptance of the technical work in people's hearts and minds.

Intent

Being organised underpins the facilitation work, which amplifies the openness and acceptance of the technical work in people's hearts and minds. Being organised is a skill set that can be learnt and is fundamental to leading productive conversations.

Reflection

How organised is your team?

Read the method card and score your team's level of maturity.

Organised

Method card

Now, read the following pages to explore the conversations required to be organised.

By practicing self-awareness and a genuine caring attitude, do your team members **regularly** have safe, open, non-judgemental and productive conversations?

| 1 | 2 | 3 | 4 | 5 |
| Never | Rarely | Sometimes | Mostly | Always |

Purpose

Central to being organised is being self-aware and ready to lead and follow people with trust and respect. It's understanding the importance of the journey from technical manager to leader.

Sincere collaboration and engagement is driven by conscious preparation, including planning and allocating time and resources, anticipating challenges, building agendas and communicating with the team.

Delivery centres around conversations that are well-structured and planned. Ground rules are set to maximise engagement and time is tracked to ensure people remain focused and on task. Real-time feedback is solicited and next steps documented.

Being organised ensures conversations are productive and meaningful.

Organised

1.1 Self-aware

Successful collaborators are self-aware and know it's all about people. They have conversations to:

- Pay attention, are respectful and genuinely interested.
- Show they're getting value from the conversation.
- Agree, differ and disagree, suggest alternatives and indicate points of interest.
- Recognise it's not about being right or wrong. There's a point in the middle that works best.
- Address conflict and negative behaviours constructively.

Common mistakes

- Not engaging in the collaboration process wholeheartedly.
- Not changing perspectives; prevents reaching an agreement.
- Underestimating the damage done to the project if people disengage.

Tools

Use these tools to become self aware:

- How to listen
- How to respond
- How to agree
- How to disagree
- How to differ
- Personal facilitation style
- Leaders launchpad

Listen

1.2 Preparation

To be confident and have productive and meaningful discussions, successful collaborators have conversations to ensure:

- Agendas give participants direction.
- Conversations are targeted and focused on the right topics.
- Sufficient time and resources are allocated to make discussions and outcomes meaningful.
- Possible risks that could derail discussions are identified and managed.
- Planning is thinking through what, when and by whom.
- Virtual meetings are business as usual, while recognising they do require more planning.
- Pre-workshop alignment by building a communications deck.

Common mistakes

- Underestimating how much work is required when planning important conversations or meetings.
- Using closed questions that solicit yes/no answers rather than open questions that solicit ideas.

Tools

Use these tools to improve preparation:

- Planning
- Facilitation estimating
- Agenda
- Virtual meetings
- Communications deck
- Questioning techniques
- Pre-workshop survey
- Facilitator clips

Prepare

1.3 Delivery

To build alignment using effective conversations, successful collaborators have conversations to:

- Ensure participants feel safe, relaxed and know why they are there.
- Allow the group to evaluate their progress against the agenda.
- Give the sponsor time to share their message and inspire people.
- Ensure conversations are targeted, focused, productive and to the point.
- Harness collective experiences and knowledge.
- Bring the workshop to a close, engendering a sense of achievement and motivation to progress.

Common mistakes

- Not documenting the next steps – all collaboration effort is linked to what happens next.
- Panicking if you are falling behind time – don't worry, as long as the discussions add value to the collaboration objectives.

Tools

Use these tools to improve delivery:

- SPACER
- Apologise upfront
- Ground rules
- Introductions
- Expectations
- Parking lot
- Breaks
- Time tracker
- Next steps
- Real time feedback
- Plus / deltas
- Wrap up
- Alignment check
- Team board

Deliver

Challenge

Out of the box

Mindset

Element

Mindset

Intent

Challenge
your mind
to sharpen
and redirect
your thinking
to generate
out-of-the-box,
provocative and
diverse ideas.

A growth mindset is fundamental to openness. It challenges your mind to sharpen and redirect your thinking in order to develop new ideas and overcome obstacles. It also generates out-of-the-box, provocative, exciting, diverse and radical ideas along with new perspectives and a sense of creative confidence.

Reflection

How is your team's mindset?

Read the method card and score your team's level of maturity.

Mindset

Mindset

Method card

Mindset

Challenge

Out of the box

Are team members **constantly** challenged to sharpen or redirect thinking to produce provocative, exciting, diverse and radical ideas?

| 1 Never | 2 Rarely | 3 Sometimes | 4 Mostly | 5 Always |

ELEMENT 2 | © TRIHEL

Now, read the following pages to explore the conversations required to have a growth mindset.

Purpose

Adopting a growth mindset drives the openness work required to ensure the use of different thinking to develop creative solutions within the technical work and acceptance work.

A growth mindset means you believe that your most basic abilities can be developed through dedication and hard work; brains and talent are just the starting point. In contrast, a fixed mindset means you believe your basic qualities, like your intelligence or talent, are simply fixed traits.

Central to a growth mindset is lifelong learning and having a beginner's mind, where you open yourself to new ideas by letting go of all preconceived notions. It's letting go of self-centred thoughts and limiting beliefs.

A growth mindset enables you to challenge and redirect your thinking away from traditional responses and to value other perspectives. It drives out-of-the-box and divergent thinking, allowing people to think differently, unconventionally and unconstrained.

A growth mindset drives different thinking, leading to different solutions and sustainable success.

Mindset

2.1 Challenge

To challenge your mind, sharpen
and redirect your thinking, effective
collaborators have conversations to:

* Avoid the temptation to go for the
  first idea; forcing you to come up with
  several others.
* Allow for incubation time by taking a
  break to do other things.
* Use vice versa thinking to be creative,
  break, with tradition and explore new
  ground.
* Understand and address psychological
  and logistical obstacles to help achieve
  goals.

Common mistakes

* Not realising the quality of any idea
  is always reflective of the ideas you
  choose to reject.
* Not allowing reflection time.
  Include incubation time into your
  work to maximise the power of the
  subconscious brain and produce
  greater insights and ideas.
* Not taking the time to map out what
  others are doing and make it relevant.

Tools

Use these tools to challenge thinking:

* Temptation
* Incubation
* Less is more
* Male / female brain
* Vice versa
* Obstacles
* Making progress

Look beyond
your own ideas

2.2 Out of the box

To generate provocative and exciting ideas with a sense of creative confidence, successful collaborators have conversations to:

- Generate new ideas by removing constraints.
- Generate new ideas by imposing constraints or specific scenarios.
- Create compelling value propositions.
- Use superpowers to drive unconstrained thinking.
- Use thinking cards as the sweet spot between structure and creativity.
- Use the value pyramid to create a compelling value proposition.

Common mistakes

- Not having a range of predefined random words or objects if teams get stuck.
- Being too serious and not having fun – ask people to imagine what could be done with superpowers.
- Underestimating how challenging fixed constraints are when generating ideas – persist, you must leave no stone unturned.

Tools

Use these tools for out of the box thinking:

- 30 circles challenge
- Random input
- Superhero
- Provocation
- Thinking cards
- Value proposition

Superpowers

"Collaboration can be taught. In most cases kids are more willing to take risks and eventually work out how to collaborate, although they need to be taught the skills for effective collaboration."

**Primary School
Principal**

Insights

Motivation

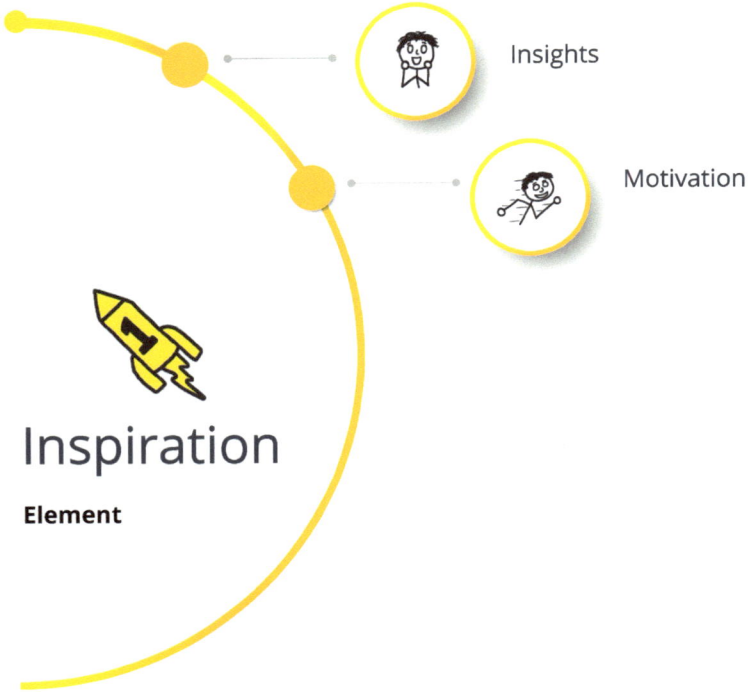

Inspiration

Element

Inspiration

Intent

Build a deeper
understanding
and desire to
change by being
motivated and
learning from
others.

Inspiration is fundamental to openness.
Inspiration builds insights into making
problem-solving creative, fun, practical,
simple and repeatable. It also establishes
a desire to change your game by being
motivated and learning from others.

Reflection

How inspired is your team?

Read the method card and score your team's level of maturity.

Inspiration

Inspiration

ELEMENT 3 | © TRIHEL...

Method card

Inspiration

Insights

Motivation

Does your team **proactively** use insights to motivate themselves, hence making problem-solving creative, fun, practical, simple and repeatable?

1	2	3	4	5
Never	Rarely	Sometimes	Mostly	Always

Now, read the following pages to explore the conversations required to inspire your team.

Purpose

Inspiration is a key driver of the openness work required to ensure the technical work and acceptance work benefit from different thinking and innovative solutions.

Inspiration builds insights to make problem-solving creative, fun, practical, simple and repeatable. It also establishes a desire to change your game by being motivated and learning from others.

Central to inspiration is insight. It's having a deeper understanding of relationships that shed light on or help solve a problem. It's that moment when a light turns on and you see a new perspective – an 'ah-ha!' moment; a new way to see the problem and solution.

Inspiration also takes advantage of the motivational forces behind people's actions and thoughts – why we behave a certain way. Learning about other people's stories and challenges generates a desire to change your own game, leading to continuous improvement.

Harnessing inspiration to provide insight and motivation energises collaborators to continuously seek effective change in their projects.

Inspiration

3.1 Insights

Effective collaborators use insights to make problem-solving creative, fun, practical, simple and repeatable. They have conversations to:

- Recognise that design thinking is a mindset, not just a process and requires diverse minds to see what's happening.
- Harness drawing as a form of visual thinking and a way to express ideas and emotions.
- Apply lateral thinking to break traditional thinking patterns and create new ideas.
- Find the sweet spot between feasibility, viability and desirability
- Help visualise an image and then draw it. With practice, your drawing will improve.

Common mistakes

- Being too serious – having fun is critical for people to be comfortable, open to creative ideas and to share.
- Overcomplicating it – keeping solutions simple can produce amazing results.
- Thinking it's easy – lateral thinking can be uncomfortable and difficult, but it will work. Creativity can be learned.

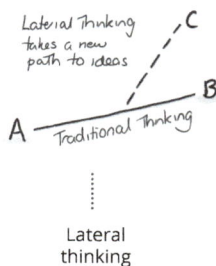

Tools

Use these tools to build insights:

- Ice challenge
- Toothpaste challenge
- Lateral thinking
- Design thinking
- Drawing stick figures

Lateral Thinking takes a new path to ideas

Traditional Thinking

A   B   C

Lateral thinking

3.2 Motivation

Successful collaborators establish a desire to change their game by being motivated and learning from others. They have conversations to:

* Explore a series of stories sharing the success factors.
* Change their game in order to continually learn, grow and remain on top of their game.
* Change traditional thinking patterns with videos to provide new ideas and perspectives.
* Use powerful stories to help people see why they must continually change their game.
* Take time to fully understand each story. This will help with delivery and impact – always reflect and have fun.
* Use inspirational videos to break our traditional thinking patterns and open us to completely new perspectives.

Common mistakes

* Rushing the stories – they provide insights that help people to think differently and reflect on their own lives and work.
* Overdoing it – have no more than three videos per day and make sure they are no longer than a few minutes, otherwise people may switch off.

Tools

Use these tools to motivate:

* Shoot for the moon
* Change your game
* Inspirational videos

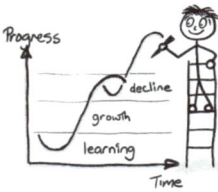

Change
your game

"Collaboration is finding the right answers. Collaboration is asking the right questions."

**Plant Operations
Manager**

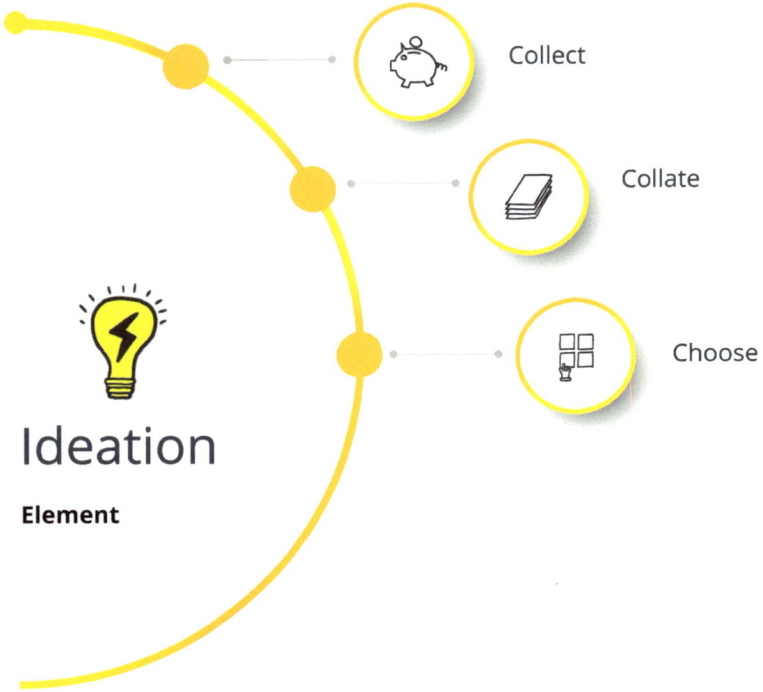

Collect

Collate

Choose

Ideation

Element

Ideation
broadens
peoples
view, builds
ownership,
ensures ideas
are not missed
and shares
accountability.

Ideation

Intent

Ideation harnesses the collective knowledge
and experience of a group and funnels
their thinking to deliver an agreed, aligned,
concise and prioritised set of actions.

Reflection

How many ideas does your team create?

Read the method card and score your team's level of maturity.

Ideation

Ideation

Ideation

Collect

Choose

Collate

ELEMENT 4 | © TRIHE

Method card

Does your team **systematically** seek to harness the group's collective knowledge to funnel thinking towards a prioritised set of actions?

1
Never

2
Rarely

3
Sometimes

4
Mostly

5
Always

Now, read the following pages to explore the conversations required to collect and prioritise ideas.

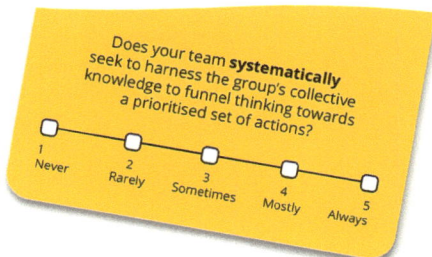

Purpose

Working in groups can produce results far beyond individual ability by:

- Broadening people's view of the world and enabling them to see another perspective.
- Building ownership, alignment and consensus of issues and their subsequent actions.
- Making sure things are not missed and, in doing so, demonstrate due diligence
- Engaging everyone and then sharing accountability.

Ideation has three parts to help funnel people's thinking:

1. **Collecting** is an open process involving brainstorming as many ideas as possible. They do not have to be in any order and no idea is a bad idea. The focus is on quantity rather than quality.
2. **Collating** is designed to remove clutter and sharpen the group's thinking. Collating overcomes team paralysis when confronted by too many options and saves significant time down the track by simplifying the prioritisation process.
3. **Choosing** continues the focusing process by filtering to elevate potential ideas to go forward with. This is done by analysing the merits of the ideas from different perspectives and testing group consensus.

Ideation

4.1 Collect

To collect ideas and ensure everyone contributes and builds on each other's ideas, successful collaborators have conversations to:

- Harness the pessimistic side of human behaviour to collect ideas.
- Agree on the question to be answered before collecting ideas.
- Welcome all ideas to ensure people are engaged and share their experience and knowledge.
- Focus on quantity of ideas rather than being bogged down on quality – that's for later.
- Capture one idea per sticker to allow for grouping and prioritising at a later stage.
- Predefine categories such as equipment, people, methods and materials.

Common mistakes

- Discussing ideas when brainstorming – the focus is to get the ideas on paper and discuss later.
- Not allocating a timeframe for brainstorming; timeframes increase energy and urgency.
- Tabling preconceived ideas; once they are out and in the open, it's very difficult to collect creative ideas.

Tools

Use these tools to collect ideas:

- Brainstorming and clarify
- Brainwaves
- Anti-brainstorming
- Nominal group technique
- Channel brainstorming
- De Bono's Thinking Hats
- Brainwriting

Brainwaves

4.2 Collate

To collate ideas, eliminate duplicates and group in common themes, effective collaborators have conversations to:

- Creatively collate and eliminate duplicate ideas.
- Organise ideas into natural themes or categories in order to overcome team paralysis brought on by too many ideas and a lack of consensus.
- Break up large group of themed ideas into smaller themes.
- Note when an idea keeps moving around, as it may belong in several themes as an individual idea.

Common mistakes

- Worrying that the process is a little slow to start. The grouping will flow once people understand the process.
- Rejecting a stand-alone idea. This idea could be as important as the others but does not fit the themes.

Tools

Use these tools to collate ideas:

- Eliminate duplicates
- Affinity grouping

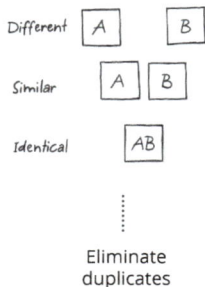

Different | A | | B |
Similar | A | B |
Identical | AB |
⋮

Eliminate duplicates

4.3 Choose

To select ideas for further consideration while maintaining consensus, successful collaborators have conversations to:

- Identify the most important ideas and where to focus energy.
- Allow the group to quickly and interactively prioritise a list to channel the groups energy and interest.
- Advocate to generate dialogue as the group considers other points of view in selecting their best option.
- Use a visual and interactive process to gain perspective by looking at a theme from different angles.
- Reduce the impact of politics and persuasive power of individual team members using must-have criteria.
- Use consensus testing to assess the degree of alignment, surface issues and concerns.

Common mistakes

- Not engaging quiet people to ensure they can contribute.
- Getting caught up in the details when selecting an idea to progress.

Tools

Use these tools to choose ideas:

- N/3
- Advocate
- Payoff matrix
- Absolute criteria screening
- Fist-to-five
- Straw poll

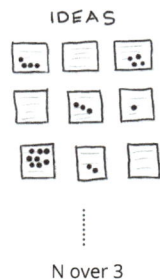

IDEAS

N over 3

*"If there's a team
of people working
towards a common goal
synergistically, no-one
gets left behind."*

Olympic Gymnast

"It's making connections and being with people. Ask any cabin crew why they do it: it's always the people."

Flight Attendant

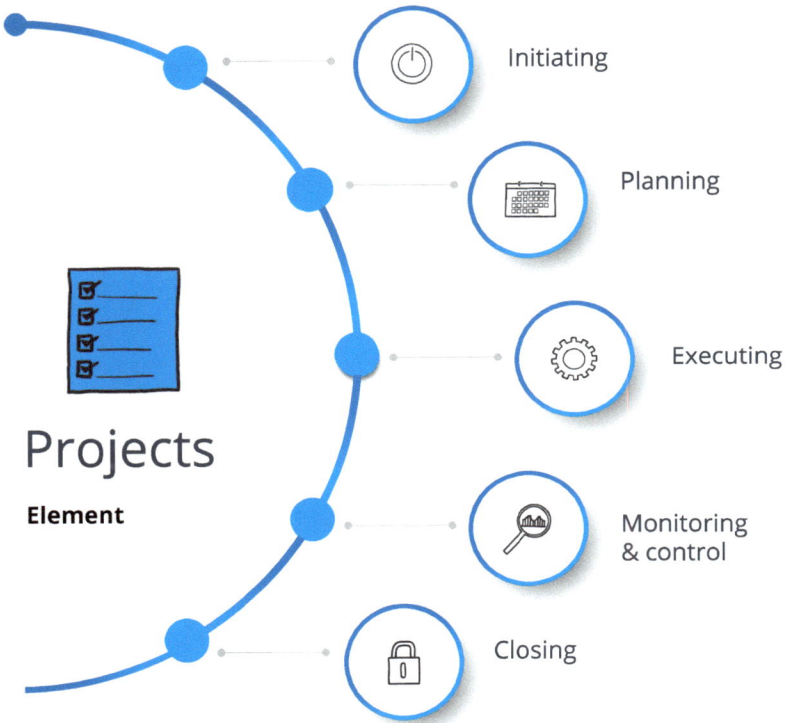

Initiating

Planning

Executing

Monitoring
& control

Closing

Projects

Element

Managing projects establishes the benefits, confirms scope, resources, timing and risks then delivers, monitors and closes out the work.

Projects

Intent

Projects describe the technical work needed to plan, organise, secure and manage resources in order to complete the goals and successfully deliver the scope as promised.

Reflection

How many projects does your team initiate and manage?

Read the method card and score your team's level of maturity.

Projects

Now, read the following pages to explore the conversations required to initiate and manage projects.

Method card

Projects

- Initiating
- Planning
- Executing
- Monitoring & control
- Closing

ELEMENT 5 | © TRIHE

Does your team **repeatedly** plan, organise, secure and manage resources for successful delivery of promised project goals?

1	2	3	4	5
Never	Rarely	Sometimes	Mostly	Always

Purpose

There are many approaches to managing projects. One method is to break down the project management process into the five specific areas (Project Management Body of Knowledge Guide 2008).

Each of these areas has a specific purpose:

1. Initiating establishes the project benefits, objectives and required work.
2. Planning confirms the scope, builds an estimate, assigns resources, sequences and schedules the work and identifies risks.
3. Executing establishes the project team and delivers the scope.
4. Monitoring and controlling generates reports on progress and manages the risks and scope.
5. Closing hands over the project and tracks the business benefits.

It's important to recognise that on major projects, the project management process runs parallel to the project lifecycle and each stage is seen as an individual project in itself.

Projects

5.1 Initiating

To establish the project's benefits, objectives and required work, leading collaborators have conversations to:

- Develop short, specific statements (project objectives) that describe the value the project will deliver.
- Identify objectives by continually asking 'why'. This moves the thinking from deliverables (a study report with recommendations) to project objective (deciding whether the project should progress).
- Provide a view of how the project work will be organised.
- Recognise that the Work Breakdown Structure (WBS) is a framework for the entire project plan to be validated and refined as you develop a deeper understanding of the project.

Common mistakes

- Rushing the development of the WBS; initially it will take time to get going and then flow quickly.
- Not involving your project team, customers, resource managers, key resources and subject matter experts when developing the WBS.

Tools

Use these tools to initiate a project:

- Project objectives
- Work breakdown structure

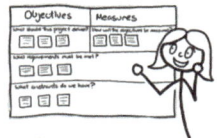

Project objectives

5.2 Planning

To confirm the scope, build an estimate, assign resources, then sequence and schedule the work and identifies risks, effective collaborators have conversations to:

- Involve your project team, their managers and experts as they have the knowledge and experience to help assign the right resources.
- For scheduling and tracking purposes, include resources even if they have no direct cost to the project.
- Sequence the work before using Microsoft Project or other tools. The sequence helps you see the workflow and enables discussions as you go.
- Keep Gantt charts simple.
- Use experienced resource providers to guide decisions about smoothing out the peak loads.
- Identify and minimise risks to protect the plan.

Common mistakes

- Not involving people who have experience in the project when brainstorming potential risks and actions.
- Not working on multiple work packages at the same time to reduce the overall duration.
- Not starting to negotiate resources as soon as possible with resource owners.

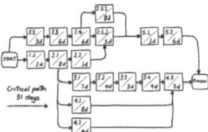

Tools

Use these tools to plan a project:

- Resource requirements
- Resource assignment
- Sequencing
- Scheduling
- Resource scheduling
- Risk assessment

Sequencing

5.3 Executing

To establish the project team and deliver the scope, successful collaborators have conversations to:

- Establish some simple ground rules upfront to eliminate confusion and frustration so people know what's expected from them and how to behave.
- Build a project induction document as part of the kick-off meeting and to induct new team members.
- Set up an environment that encourages and enables joint problem-solving and collaboration across the team and other stakeholders.

Common mistakes

- Not engaging new team members and bringing them up to speed on the project principles.
- Assuming people know what is expected without clear ground rules.

Tool

Use this tools to execute a project:

- Starting the project

Starting point

5.4 Monitoring and controlling

To report on progress and manage the risks and scope, effective collaborators have conversations to:

- Track actual project performance against the project plan.
- Keep the scorecard simple and use colours to help the team focus on what's important and what needs constant attention.
- Communicate project performance information consistently and regularly to stakeholders.
- Identify when the project scope changes and ensure the plan is kept current to reflect changes in scope.
- Monitor critical parts of the project plan more frequently than other parts.

Common mistakes

- Not having scope changes (also called variations) approved by the sponsor before they are added to the project.
- Not addressing a change in scope when it does not immediately impact the project schedule or approach.
- Accepting extra work and either running out of money, delivering late or producing a poor quality product.

Tools

Use these tools to monitor and control a project:

- Monitoring and reporting
- Scope change management

Monitoring & Reporting

5.5 Closing

To hand over the project and track the business benefits, leading collaborators have conversations to:

- Review project outcomes and evaluate the project business case.
- Capture learnings for future projects.
- Celebrate project success.
- Establish benefits realisation tracking and the reporting process.
- Compile project handover documentation.
- Know that a good transition will include a handover from the project team to operations, including all pertinent information so that the project's success can continue to be monitored and realised.

Common mistakes

- Not including the project team or creating a positive environment. This significantly limits the value of the lesson learnt exercise.
- Not including closeout and evaluation activities in your project plan and budget.
- Not checking whether the documents need to be updated to reflect the current state of play, or revised to be clearer to someone outside of the team.

Tools

Use these tools to close out a project:

- Project closure and evaluation
- Project handover

Project handover

Improvement Element

Define

Measure

Analyse

Improve

Business improvement takes an opportunity from start to finish in order to realise its benefits within the business.

Improvement

Intent

Improvement describes the technical work needed to take an opportunity from conception through to realising its benefits when institutionalised within the business.

Reflection

How does your team implement improvements?

Read the method card and score your team's level of maturity.

Improvement

Method card

Improvement

- Define
- Measure
- Analyse
- Improve

How **successfully** does your team take an idea from 'start to finish' to realise the benefits in the business?

| 1 Never | 2 Rarely | 3 Sometimes | 4 Mostly | 5 Always |

ELEMENT 6 | © TRIHE

Now, read the following pages to explore the conversations required to implement improvements.

Purpose

There are many methodologies designed specifically to deliver business improvement. We have chosen to use the Six Sigma Define, Measure, Analyse, Improve, Control (DMAIC) methodology.

This methodology has five phases:

1. **Define** phase describes the improvement idea and sets clear boundaries and goals. It transfers ownership from the project sponsor to the business improvement team.
2. **Measure** phase builds trust and openness by using data to identify the top improvement opportunities to be analysed.
3. **Analyse** phase identifies root causes and effective solutions to realise the improvement benefits.
4. **Improve** phase identifies change impacts on the business and ensures people are capable, ready and communicated with to adopt the project solutions.
5. **Control** phase ensures the benefits are tracked and realised within the business.

We are not mandating an improvement methodology or describing how they work. There are some great books already published that can systematically inform how to deliver projects using Six Sigma.

Improvement

6.1 Define

To describe the improvement idea and set clear boundaries and goals, successful collaborators have conversations to:

- Identify the benefits the project will deliver as the foundation of the business case.
- Develop a statement that explains the characteristics of the problem or opportunity in order to focus the team and communicate project goals.
- Clearly define what's in/out of scope and put people at ease by knowing the boundaries.
- Develop a visual picture of the process the project is aiming to improve.
- Engage the workforce and key stakeholders from the beginning.
- Complete a summary charter at the end of the project definition phase to bring together all the thinking into a well-structured framework.

Common mistakes

- Ignoring people's anger regarding possible changes. It is important to be patient, calm and attentive. Do not get into a debate.
- Long-winded opportunity statements that don't include data to help quantify what is being addressed or outline potential business benefits.
- Rushing the chartering process.

Tools

Use these tools to define improvement:

- Benefits realisation
- Project charter
- Opportunity statement
- What's in/out of scope
- SIPOC tool
- Engaging the workforce

Define
scope

6.2 Measure

To build trust, openness and identify opportunities for improvement, effective collaborators have conversations to:

- Build trust and openness by responding to people's questions and concerns.
- Share detailed specific context around the project.
- Categorise possible opportunities using tools like the fishbone to build a solid understanding of what's happening.
- Map possible data sources relating to primary metrics.
- Build a visual picture of possible opportunities for improvement, being careful not to assign blame as the workforce interprets the data.
- Build a master opportunity list spreadsheet as the central summary of all the decisions and continually refine it to identify the top opportunities.

Common mistakes

- Expecting all the answers early in the project; this happens as the analysis phase progresses.
- Not making someone accountable for providing and sourcing the data; otherwise it will not happen.

Tools

Use these tools to identify improvement opportunities:

- Surfacing the tough questions
- Detailed context
- Opportunity driver fishbone
- Seven wastes
- Data map
- Data posters
- Master opportunity list
- Information café

Data map

6.3 Analyse

To apply effective solutions that realise improvement benefits, successful collaborators have conversations to:

- Use the fishbone to identify and prioritise possible causes prior to root cause analysis.
- Employ a process map as a means and not an end; it's a work in progress – often messy at the beginning. Be patient as you refine and improve results.
- Agree on the analysis framework before undertaking discussions to ensure conversations are consistent and structured.
- Conduct one-on-one interviews to hear different responses to the same question and understand what is really happening.
- Build ownership of the results by allowing people to hear the questions and answers as a combined group.

Common mistakes

- Not spending time upfront to understand the business so that people's responses are pertinent to the problem.
- Making the findings difficult for others to understand.

Tools

Use these tools to analyse improvement opportunities:

- Root cause analysis
- Process mapping
- Framework driven discussions
- PAST cast
- SWOT analysis
- PESTEL analysis

Process mapping

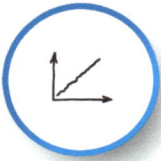

6.4 Improve

To identify the impacts of change and to ensure people are capable, ready and communicated with, effective collaborators have conversations to

- Identify the impact and timing of changes the improvement will bring to the organisation.
- Ensure the project plan activities reflect these changes and a successful transition to the future state.
- Train and transfer the skills and knowledge to people so the improvement outcomes can be adopted and the benefits realised.
- Establish a communications strategy for the development and execution of communications.
- Remember the four elements of adult learning: tell me, show me through demonstrations, let me do it hands on and support me.
- Communicate using a positive and supportive tone and respond to questions or feedback promptly.

Common mistakes

- Thinking the change impacts are stationary, when in fact they become clearer with each phase of the project.
- Not communicating critical messages multiple times.
- Assuming the training will just happen and not allocating sufficient time and resources.

Tools

Use these tools to deliver improvements:

- Change impact assessment
- Training strategy and plan
- Communication strategy and plant

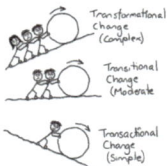

Transformational change (complex)

Transitional Change (Moderate

Transactional Change (Simple)

Assess change impact

"Collaboration is building off each other's strengths to cooperate as a team."

Year 6 Student

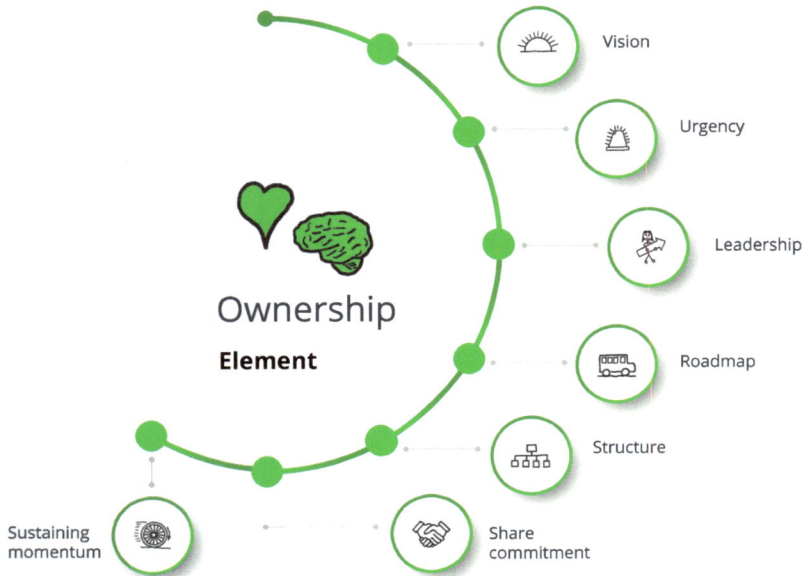

Ownership Element

Vision

Urgency

Leadership

Roadmap

Structure

Share commitment

Sustaining momentum

Ownership

Intent

Traditionally, we focus on the technical solutions and assume the solution will be accepted.

Ownership ensures that all the technical work is undertaken meaningfully and accepted by everyone. It engages and excites people at a subconscious level to be a part of the work.

Reflection

What is your teams level of ownership?

Read the method card and score your team's level of maturity.

Ownership

Now, read the following pages to explore the conversations required to ensure strong ownership.

Ownership

Ownership

Vision

Structure

Urgency

Share commitment

Leadership

Sustaining momentum

Roadmap

ELEMENT 7 | © TRIHEL

Method card

Is your team **totally** committed to ensuring all technical work is undertaken meaningfully and accepted in people's 'hearts and minds' at a sub-conscious level?

1 Never — 2 Rarely — 3 Sometimes — 4 Mostly — 5 Always

Purpose

Ownership is intangible and can't be held. It's about people's beliefs and behaviours. Mistakenly, teams assume that the technical work will ensure assimilation of behaviours, but it's often not the case. Think of ownership as a framework called the "Ownership Wheel". The wheel has seven elements to be continuously worked on to ensure the technical work is being accepted.

The elements are:

1. **A Vision** that provides a clear view of what life will be like after the collaboration.
2. **Urgency** that makes the collaboration real, right now and drives action.
3. **Leadership** that sets an example to generate enthusiasm and encourage the team to embrace the work.
4. **A Road Map** that provides a strategy for achieving the vision and overall direction.
5. **A Structure** that ensures the systems, tools and resources are available to do the work.
6. **Shared Commitment** that ensures the team understands what is in it for them.
7. **Sustaining Momentum** that recognises hurdles, continuously energises and celebrates success.

The truth is that if people don't want to be part of the collaboration – then it is doomed. So, the team must continually work on engaging people and demonstrating how their contribution will benefit them and others.

Ownership

7.1 Vision

To provide a clear view of what life will be like after the work, successful collaborators have conversations to:

- Develop a picture that appeals to both the "head" and the "heart".
- Create "outside-in" points of view (I.e. what would the customer see more/less of?).
- Create a bold and clear sense of purpose that inspires and energises others "beyond self".
- Engage people in translating and giving meaning to the vision for their piece of the world (i.e. behavioural and actionable).

Common mistakes

- "Inside-Out" where the vision is focused internally, not on the external demands and opportunities of customers, technology and socio-political trends.
- Factions with no buy-in on the direction; not everyone supports the vision in private talks.
- Confusion where the vision is too complex or abstract to understand and translate into action easily.

Tools

Use these tools create a vision:

- Mapping the change
- Elevator speech
- Project principles
- Project tagline
- Aspirations

Vision

7.2 Urgency

To make the work real, right now and drive action, effective collaborators have conversations to:

- Define the project's importance and urgency to multiple stakeholders.
- Establish the "case for change".
- Generate the energy needed to get the project and change kicked off.
- Generate external or internal data to induce change (e.g. reports, surveys, benchmarks).
- Demonstrate best practice site visits and personal examples.
- Command new performance levels (customers, internal management, regulatory).

Common mistakes

- Failure to build team consensus on the need for the project change.
- Assumption that the need is obvious to all or "they" just don't get it.
- Shallow diagnosis (symptoms vs. root cause).

Tools

Use these tools to create urgency:

- Threats vs opportunity matrix
- FAST matrix

Urgency

7.3 Leadership

To generate enthusiasm and encourage the team to embrace the work, outstanding collaborators have conversations to:

- Ensure strong leadership for the project and effective change.
- Establish clear expectations with accountability for accomplishing the project and change.
- Continuously pay attention to the project and feel energized by change.
- Focus on the "critical few" priorities, "Known for...' or "Cares about...".
- Match time allocation to stated priorities (i.e. pitches in).
- Ensure accountability for action items and use metrics to track and reward performance.

Common mistakes

- Leaders shift to other goals before completing the initiative ("flavour of the month").
- Leaders fail to integrate or link the project and subsequent change initiative with the "real work" and imperatives of the business.
- Leaders rely on the brilliance of the technical work instead of acceptance by the stakeholders.

Tools

Use this tool to create leadership:

- Leadership assessment

Leadership

7.4 Roadmap

To provide a strategy for achieving the vision and overall direction, leading collaborators have conversations to:

- Develop a transition road map to enhance the ability to reward key events and milestones.
- Establish accurate measures to provide focus, direction and momentum.
- Take corrective action (which can only occur if you know you are off track).
- Tie results to business goals (e.g. growth, safety, productivity) and articulate them in concrete terms.
- Develop milestones and measures to track progress on the technical work and acceptance.
- Hold people accountable for their commitments and results.

Common mistakes

- Great plan, but no accountabilities assigned on the review process.
- Tollgates address only the technical issues – no acceptance measures included.
- No measures of success, so no progress indicators.

Tools

O penness
T echnical
A cceptance

Use this tool to create a roadmap:

- Critical 'T and A' milestones and measures

Milestones
and measures

7.5 Structure

To ensure the necessary systems, tools and resources, effective collaborators have conversations to:

- Organise, hire, develop, reward, compensate, access information and allocate resources.
- Realign the "organisational infrastructure" to enable people to be successful.
- Rigorously evaluate the degree to which our project will depend on changes in our current systems and structures.
- Identify which systems and structures are the biggest "levers" to drive change.
- Are early to involve the "owners" of the systems that will make the change last.
- Plan early for downstream changes.

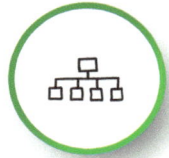

Common mistakes

- Lack of assessment on whether the intended changes will be supported or inhibited by existing systems and structures.
- Failure to address the power of faulty measures and incongruent reward systems creates cynicism and "gamesmanship" rather than initiative and leadership.
- Failing to anticipate the need for training, information systems or changes in job design – factors that impact the daily success of people.

Tools

Use this tool to create structure:

- Structure for change

Change structure

7.6 Shared commitment

To establish what is in it for the team and to actively engage resistance, successful collaborators have conversations to:

- Understand key stakeholders whose support and commitment will "make or break" the effort.
- Influence the critical mass using positive interest-based strategies.
- Monitor the pulse of commitment and resistance to remain proactive on this critical work.
- Leverage sponsors to form a network of support.
- Determine who will resist and the sources of resistance and deploy effective "work through" strategies.
- Engage in appropriate problem-solving and win-win conflict resolution activities.

Common mistakes

- Failing to recognise and work with resistance, underestimating it.
- Assuming that technical work and "logic" are sufficient to generate buy-in.
- Not involving others because of perceived time constraints.

Tools

Use these tools to create shared commitment:

- Resistance to change
- Stakeholder analysis
- Engagement strategy
- Effective communication
- Communication plan
- Communication protocols
- Managing expectations
- Performance system analysis
- Cartoonist

Resistance
to change

7.7 Sustaining momentum

To recognise hurdles, continuously energise and celebrate success, leading collaborators have conversations to:

- Ensure project success by providing the resources and support needed for the life of the project.
- Create awareness of enablers and identify barriers to sustained change and action items to address.
- Integrate multiple initiatives into a common focus that drives results, focuses energy and publicises early wins.
- Run many small experiments and capture the learning from success and failure.
- Transfer learning from one site to another.
- Leverage symbols, language and culture to support the change – including promotions and new employees.

Common mistakes

- Waiting for the "perfect" solution before acting.
- Resources are "front-loaded" and not allocated to the team for the life of the project.
- Measure, reward and promote the old way while espousing the new way.

Tools

Use these tools to sustain momentum:

- Force field analysis
- Force field analysis in groups
- Momentum wheel
- Team effectiveness assessment

Celebrate success

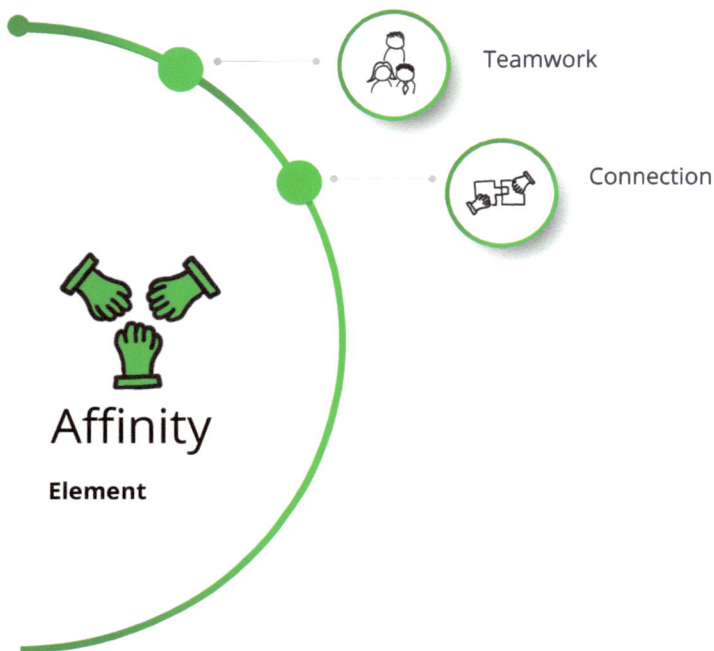

Teamwork

Connection

Affinity

Element

Affinity

Intent

Effective collaboration builds affinity and is driven by honesty, trust and respect.

Affinity builds acceptance by ensuring that all the technical work is undertaken meaningfully by everyone. It brings people together from different backgrounds and cultures to share knowledge, experience and combine their efforts to solve problems.

Reflection

Is your team connected?

Read the method card and score your team's level of maturity.

Affinity

Affinity

Teamwork

Connection

ELEMENT 8 | © TRIHELI

Method card

Now, read the following pages to explore the conversations required to build teamwork and connections.

Does your team **constantly** embrace people from different backgrounds and cultures to share knowledge and experience to solve problems?

1	2	3	4	5
Never	Rarely	Sometimes	Mostly	Always

Purpose

Collaboration is not easy as it requires people to see a bigger picture, a view of the world beyond their own. People must be prepared to engage and listen while putting aside personal preferences for the benefit of the team and business.

Collaboration requires strong teamwork and does not happen by itself. A business needs to make sufficient time for collaboration and establish structures that foster sharing and working together.

It's important to recognise that collaboration and conflict are intertwined. Effective collaboration relies on people coming together with diverse and different perspectives – this is where the magic happens. It's completely normal for people to disagree and have conflict. How you manage conflict is what leads to a positive and fruitful collaboration.

Collaboration is built on honesty and trust. People trust those who perform reliably and competently and display concern for the wellbeing of others. People must connect while recognising and valuing differences. Open and transparent communication is fundamental if the team is to develop and collaborate.

Affinity

8.1 Teamwork

To build effective teamwork, successful collaborators have conversations to:

- Systematically collaborate and work together on a virtual platform.
- Celebrate diversity of thinking as being fundamental for an effective team.
- Recognise, foster and engage in team differences.
- Involve people within and external to the business.
- Accept conflict is normal as the first step in building a foundation for collaboration and teamwork.
- See that virtual teams are the future, recognizing challenges as opportunities to develop the team and deliver superior outcomes.

Common mistakes

- Assuming collaboration will just happen– like all things, it takes time.
- Not having the technology to enable teams to collaborate effectively.

Tools

Use these tools to build teamwork:

- Collaborative enterprise
- Conflict & collaboration
- Collaboration types
- Brain based collaboration
- Trust in virtual teams

Collaborative enterprise

8.2 Connection

To be open and honest and collaborate effectively, leading collaborators have conversations to:

- Connect at a "hearts and minds" (sub-conscious) level.
- Know oneself, their colleagues and show empathy.
- Celebrate and foster cultural diversity.
- Trust people who perform reliably and competently and display concern for the wellbeing of others.
- Build "trust into the project by understanding the stages of team development.
- Understand the challenges of multicultural team, which is fundamental for a motivated and effective, culturally- diverse team.

Common mistakes

- Assuming team connections happen by themselves.
- Believing that everyone connects in the same way.

Tools

Use these tools to build connection:

- Building connections with images
- Team preferences
- Team profile
- Team development
- Cultural awareness
- Multicultural teams
- High performance teams

Cultural
awareness

Success profile

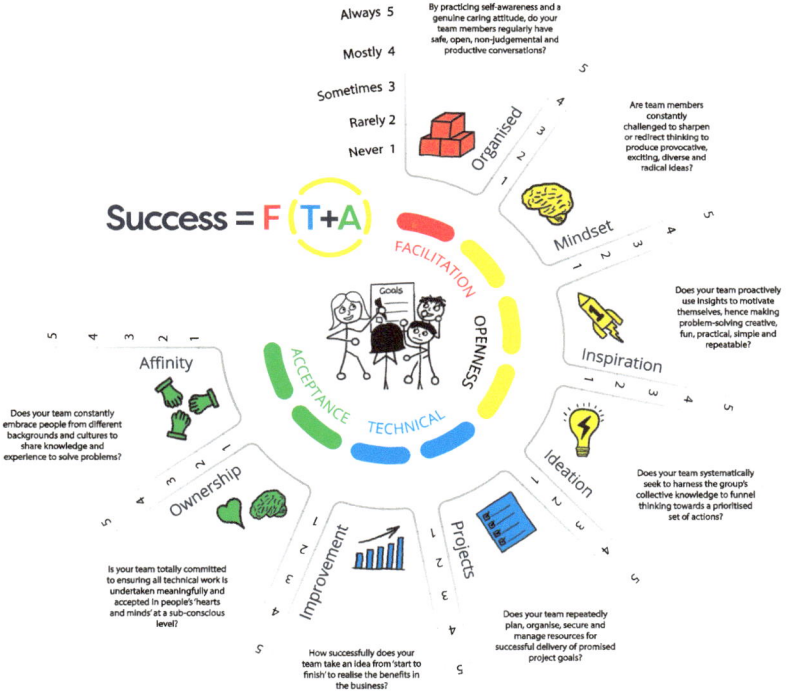

Success = F(T+A)

Always 5
Mostly 4
Sometimes 3
Rarely 2
Never 1

By practicing self-awareness and a genuine caring attitude, do your team members regularly have safe, open, non-judgemental and productive conversations?

Are team members constantly challenged to sharpen or redirect thinking to produce provocative, exciting, diverse and radical ideas?

Does your team proactively use insights to motivate themselves, hence making problem-solving creative, fun, practical, simple and repeatable?

Does your team systematically seek to harness the group's collective knowledge to funnel thinking towards a prioritised set of actions?

Does your team repeatedly plan, organise, secure and manage resources for successful delivery of promised project goals?

How successfully does your team take an idea from 'start to finish' to realise the benefits in the business?

Is your team totally committed to ensuring all technical work is undertaken meaningfully and accepted in people's 'hearts and minds' at a sub-conscious level?

Does your team constantly embrace people from different backgrounds and cultures to share knowledge and experience to solve problems?

Organised

Mindset

Inspiration

Ideation

Projects

Improvement

Ownership

Affinity

FACILITATION

OPENNESS

TECHNICAL

ACCEPTANCE

Goals

Reflection

1. Reflect on the element, sub-element, intent, drivers and common mistakes.
2. Score your team from 'rarely' to 'without fail' for each element.
3. Transfer your scores onto the Success Profile.
4. Create a team profile from your own perspective.
5. Identify which elements require work to improve your team's overall success.
6. Ask your colleagues to take the survey to create an overall team profile.
7. As a team, discuss the results, reflecting on the sub-element, intent, drivers and common mistakes in order to build a deeper understanding of the results.
8. Confirm which elements require work to improve your team's overall success.
9. Review the focus sub-element's respective conversation tools and select a few to improve your overall success.
10. Schedule some time with your team to apply the key tools.
11. Create an action list using the tool to improve your team.

Scan to view and download the complete resource pack.

**Preparedness
Method Cards**

**Idea Generation
Method Cards**

**Project Management
Method Cards**

**Ownership & Affinity
Method Cards**

**Team Success
Poster**

All resources are located at www.trihelix.com.au/resources

Imagine collaborating
with the best

Closing thoughts

Collaborating with diverse people to build a community with lasting connections and shared goals to truly make a difference is why we get up in the morning. Embracing the digital world with confidence has enabled us to realise success with faster turnarounds and more effective work sessions while maintaining a work/life balance.

To make this transition we must actively confront unknowns and engage with changes in technology and ensure all participants feel connected and empowered. We must commit to travel less, thus reducing costs and CO_2 emissions while reclaiming our valuable personal time to use as we please.

Importantly our research found that our desire to collaborate is part of our DNA - a law of nature. It is hardwired into our brains and essential to our survival. It makes us feel good as we connect with our thoughts and emotions. Collaboration is powered by people, through our interactions. The end game is collaboration produces ideas and ideas change and evolve humanity.

Reduce costs and CO_2
emissions and reclaim
personal time

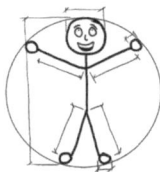

Collaboration is part of
our human design

The future of collaboration will be digital. We will use our digital devices to communicate and interact to produce ideas, alignment, connections, engagement and results. Work will be completed synchronously online, in real-time, regardless of our location and time zone. Work will also be completed asynchronously using shared documents around the clock, independently of each other.

Future of collaboration will be digital

Collaboration in a digital world takes the form of a campaign of short, focused interactions spaced over several weeks or months. Using this approach helps to manage and guide collaborators over time and across varied digital platforms while maintaining transparency, engagement and a common purpose.

Look at collaboration as a campaign

Our collaboration mantras guide any successful digital collaboration, we must: strive to work in parallel to maximize collaboration; always over prepare and over prepare; design collaboration as series of sprints; seek to be visual in everything we do; and constantly change our game to be on top of our game.

Make collaboration mantras part of you day

Embrace collaboration
essentials

Campaign involvement
drives interactions

Maximize the rewards
manage the threats

Our collaboration essentials underpin the mantras and are a necessary first step to collaborating in a digital world. As individuals we must foster a digital mind, apply the art of facilitation and actively use digital collaboration platforms like whiteboards.

A typical collaboration campaign will be a blend of three interactions spaced over time , starting virtual, then hybrid, possibly face to face and closing with virtual. The types of interactions are in response to stakeholder diversity and numbers, geography and relationship building. Spacing the interactions contributes to a campaign's success as people can incubate and reflect, creating new insights into the problem.

When designing a collaboration campaign, our goal is to maximise the rewards and manage the threats people experience.

The collaboration scope is fundamental to a campaign design and describes what milestones and deliverables are expected to be included. Will the collaboration produce ideas, alignment, connections, engagement or results or a combination of all these outcomes. A bigger scope will increase the campaign timeline. Always develop the scope upfront with the collaboration team as this builds confidence, motivation and a common purpose.

Collaboration scope sets boundaries

Successful collaborations engage in various types of conversations. Open conversations empower people to think differently. Conversations around the technical work support the project outcomes. Acceptance conversations build ownership and engagement in the team. The relationship between the various types of conversations required for a successful collaboration is our success formula. Any inbalance in types of conversations help to form the scope of collaboration.

Types of conversations

This book provides links to method cards and 150 tools that guide you through every step required to deliver a successful collaboration campaign.

Method card and tools

"What you bring to the collaboration, is not what you say or do, but rather the energy you bring to uplift people."

Yoga Instructor

www.ingramcontent.com/pod-product-compliance
Lightning Source LLC
Chambersburg PA
CBHW041006210326
41597CB00001B/25